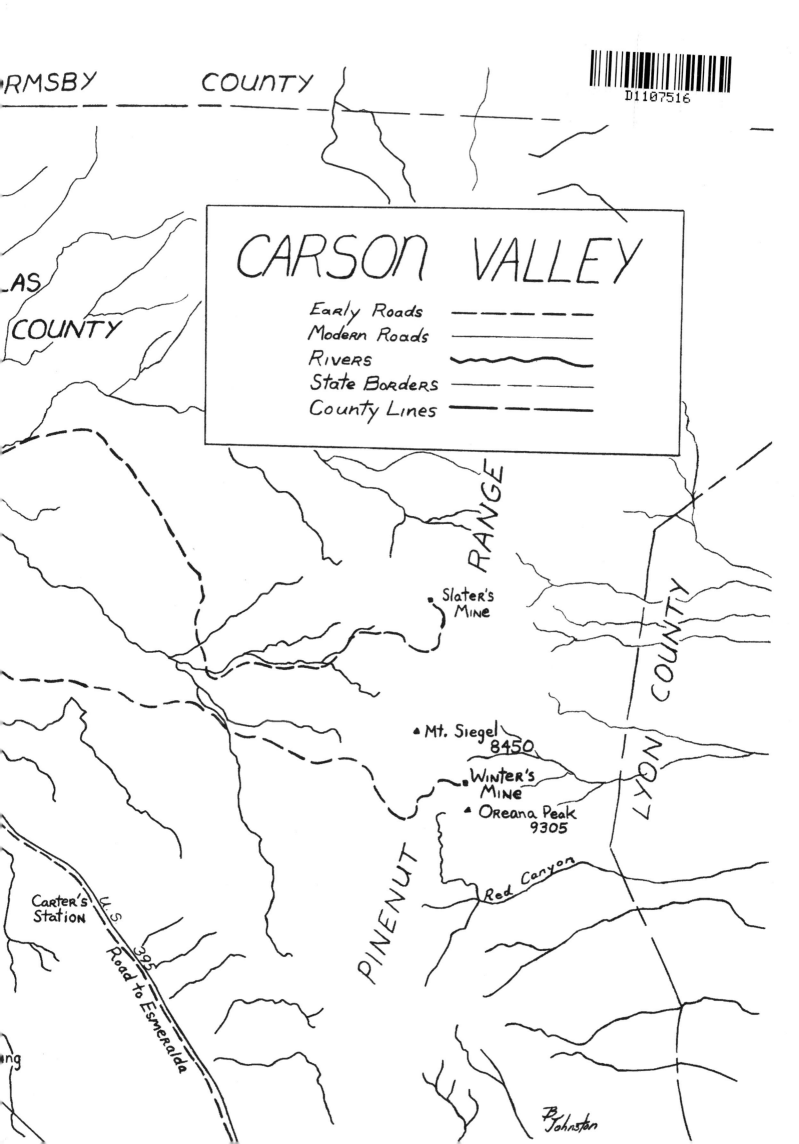

RMSBY   COUNTY

LAS

COUNTY

CARSON VALLEY

Early Roads   — — — —
Modern Roads   ————————
Rivers   ~~~~~~
State Borders   ————————
County Lines   —— — ——

RANGE

. Slater's
  Mine

LYON COUNTY

▲ Mt. Siegel
  8450

■ Winter's
  Mine

▲ Oreana Peak
  9305

PINENUT

Red Canyon

Carter's
Station

U.S. 395

Road to Esmeralda

ng

B Johnston

Francesca,

It was a pleasure to meet you. I know you will do very well in your new job.

Oh, Canada!

Published 2002 by
THE CARSON VALLEY HISTORICAL SOCIETY
with a grant from
THE GRACE DANGBERG FOUNDATION, INC.
All proceeds from this book go to
The Carson Valley Historical Society.

First Printing 1972, 1000
Second Printing 1973, 2000
Third Printing 1979, 2000
Fourth Printing 1991, 1000
Fifth Printing 2002, 1000

Printed by Central Plains Book Manufacturing, Winfield, KS

CARSON VALLEY

Historical Sketches of Nevada's First Settlement

GRACE DANGBERG

Acknowledgements

We of the Carson Valley Historical Society acknowledge with sincere appreciation the support and interest of all you who have contributed to the making of this first book about Carson Valley. Many of you and your forebears have been named. Others not named are included in this acknowledgement. May your stories be the substance of other books.

A special word of gratitude goes to Yvonne Saddler of the Douglas County Library for the many services only a competent librarian can afford the writer of a book. Special mention must also be made of Eva Scarselli and Frank L. Griffin, Jr. for guidance in giving the text its final form.

G. D.

Contents

INTRODUCTION

ARSON VALLEY, just over the eastern crest of the Sierra Nevada from Lake Tahoe, shares the natural beauty of the famous lake and adds to the attractions of nature the distinction of being Nevada's first settlement. Through this valley ran the last segment of the California Trail to be opened up between Salt Lake City and Sacramento, a shorter and more easily traveled road than its nearest rival, the Donner Pass road to the north. Overshadowed by the stirring events that succeeded the discovery of gold in 1849 is the fact that this twenty-odd mile segment became a part of a transcontinental route long envisioned by Thomas H. Benton (United States Senator from Missouri 1820-1850) who, in 1819, began a campaign for a North American Road to India.

Thus, this isolated valley, lying on the western rim of the Great Basin and in the shadow of the Sierra Nevada Mountains may be seen to have entered momentarily the mainstream of national history and of world commerce. Extravagant claims, one may say, for a small area that, until the middle of the last century, had not been traversed by any known white man or explorer and whose only inhabitants were the Washoe Indians, a tribe who were, in 1850, still living in the Stone Age.

The importance of this segment of the California Trail, called in its day the Carson River Route, was widely recognized during the years of its heavy use from 1848, the year of its discovery by Bigler, to 1869 when the driving of the golden spike (or was it silver?) at Promontory Point wiped out its advantage as the shortest road from Salt Lake City to Sacramento. Thenceforward, the Central and Union Pacific railroads enjoyed this distinction.

Descriptions of the road through Carson Valley by those who traveled it range all the way from noting the blue flax that grew along the trail to designating the valley the "paradise of quadrapeds." This was the sobriquet given it by the correspondent of the *San Francisco Herald* who lived in Genoa from 1857 to 1861. Indeed, the very fact that the *Herald*, after publishing accounts of the happenings in Carson Valley for a number of years, at length saw fit to place a correspondent there for weekly reports testifies to the importance of the road and the community of Carson Valley in the days of the pioneers. Furthermore, no writer on the great American migration of the fifties fails to give the crossing of the Sierra Nevada via Carson Valley a prominent place in his work.

During the period of its use, first the government of California and then that of the United States took notice of the importance of the Carson River Route.* In 1855, the Surveyor General of California commissioned Sherman Day and George Goddard to survey the approaches to the valley and its road with a view to the construction and improvement of an immigrant wagon road. Three years later (in 1858) Captain Simpson of the Corps of Topographical Engineers of the United States Army was commissioned to explore a direct wagon road from Camp Floyd, Utah, to Genoa, Carson Valley. He accomplished this assignment in 1859.

In view of these facts, Carson Valley held a unique place in the annals of the west for nearly 20 years or until 1869 when the transcontinental railroad was completed. The valley's written records are almost complete from 1851 to the present. Testimony taken in early water disputes provides significant comments and evidence as to the character of the pioneers and the scope of their activities. The fact that a number of them and/or their descendants from time to time took the opportunity offered by the local weekly paper to record their reminiscences is an added source of information.

Glimpses of the volume of traffic on the Carson River Route between 1852 and 1859 (as reported to the *San Francisco Herald*) supply the factual basis for its place in history.

In the *Herald* for June 15, 1852, one observer reported that many families from Salt Lake waited in Carson Valley for the snow to go off the mountains so they could proceed into the Sacramento Valley with their teams.

In the same issue, another observer saw pack trains on the streets of California towns being loaded with provisions, liquors, etc., to take to the immigrants. A large herd of horses was on the way to Carson Valley where the owner could exchange fresh horses with immigrants for weary and broken down stock. Seven hundred and twenty horses and mules crossed the new bridge over the South Fork of the American River on the *new* Carson Valley route.

In the August 13, 1853 issue, quoting from the *Deseret News*, the paper reported that in late May of 1853 no less than a thousand wagons and 300,000 head of stock were on the road between the Humboldt and Carson Valley.

The immigrants were mostly families with large herds

---

*The Carson River Route was also called the "emigrant trail." This calls for clarification of the use of the words emigrant and immigrant in pioneer days. The migrants from east of the Mississippi thought and spoke of themselves as emigrants from the states. When these same people entered California they were spoken of as immigrants.

of cattle, numbering one to eight hundred to the train, as reported in the September 28, 1854 *Herald*. The informant could make no estimate of the number of cattle but stated there were about 10,000 sheep.

One observer of traffic reported in the August 25, 1857 issue that from the Humboldt to the upper Brockliss Station (on the American River near Pacific House, Eldorado County, California) there was an uninterrupted chain . . . the wagons in sight of each other all the way . . . the great body of immigrants was coming by way of Carson Valley . . . as far as was known there were 25,000 head of cattle and from 2000 to 3000 head of horses and mules.

On January 2, 1859, it was reported that Carson Valley was the favorite route of the immigrants. In September of 1859 one observer saw a single drove of 744 mules. Later in the month the numbers of immigrants in only two wagon trains were counted: in the one were 300 men, 124 women, 262 children, 80 horses, 63 mules, 1718 cattle, and 60 wagons. In the other train of 92 wagons were 283 men, 79 women, 48 children, 67 horses, 39 mules and 7367 cattle (issues of September 3 and 14, 1859).

Also in the September 3 issue, an observer in Genoa watched 36 wagon loads of immigrants pass his window as he wrote a letter.

In the history of Carson Valley we have before us a microcosm of the rise and fall of civilizations. The rise may be illustrated in the history of the three principal towns of the valley (Genoa, Gardnerville, and Minden) and the fall may be illustrated in the disappearance of the numerous hamlets which were left to decay when business and trade forsook them. Genoa, on the Carson River Route, flourished from 1850 to 1869; the peak was reached during the years 1858 to 1869 when the mines on the Comstock were booming, and seven-tenths of the freight from California to Virginia City was passing through the town. Gardnerville began in 1879 as a place for servicing the teams and wagons hauling valley produce to booming Bodie. Minden, upon the completion of a branch of the Virginia and Truckee Railway in 1905, became a shipping point for supplies on the road to booming Tonopah and Goldfield.

Genoa had several brief periods of prosperity after 1869 then entered long years of decline beginning in the early 1890s, only to revive during the present era of expansion in recreation that is now engulfing Carson Valley. Gardnerville and Minden, although passing through the doldrums on several occasions, have continued to flourish.

The hamlets that have decayed and disappeared are Mottsville, Sheridan, Fairview, Centerville and Waterloo.

The circumstances in which these changes have taken place are related in the sketches which follow. These are set down in the mood and often in the vernacular in which they were told by the observer or the actors themselves in the minor dramas.

(Courtesy Frank L. Griffin, Jr.)

X

THE CARSON RIVER ROUTE, A WAGON WAY WEST

Discovery — Approaching Carson Valley From the West

BEYOND THE long shaded spur on the left of the picture below lies the "dark defile" now known as Woodford's Canyon. Down this rugged, rock-strewn chasm came the first white men to enter Carson Valley. This was in August of 1848. They were a small party of Mormons, members of the Mormon Battalion, led by Henry W. Bigler. These men had been called back to Zion (Salt Lake City) by Brigham Young. They were commissioned at Sutter's Fort on the Sacramento to open up a wagon road over the Sierra Nevada to replace the one over Donner Pass which was plagued by fourteen crossings of the Truckee River.

Appropriately Bigler called the West Fork of the Carson River, along the banks of which his road led, the Pilot River. It took one week to put a road through the seven-miles-long Woodford's Canyon; the labor was hard, the surroundings lovely — forest with undergrowth of blue flax — and there was good trout fishing in the river!

Bigler's road crew followed the "Pilot River" down its course in the shadow of the Sierra Nevada Mountains, through a valley which he estimated to be twelve miles wide. Plenty of grass grew there where, in 1848, the antelope roamed. They killed one. This was Carson Valley.

Some Indians came into their camp and that night the mountains appeared to be "all on fire;" the air was full of smoke. The next day was Sunday. The party continued on down the valley, past the springs (later named Walley Hot Springs) and then over sandy ground where little grass

Behind the long, dark spur on the left is Woodford's Canyon. *(Courtesy of Juanita Schubert)*

Giant boulders in the "dark defile" as the Carson (Woodford's) Canyon was described by those who first passed through it. *(Courtesy of Frank L. Griffin, Jr.)*

grew. Finally they passed through wild sage and again the lovely blue flax flowers were, he says, "in abundance." That Sunday night the Indians made a hundred fires on the mountains. Why? Bigler stated, "for what I do not know." His guide, however, said a smoke raised on the mountains was a sign of peace and a token for help; he said a smoke in the valley was for war. Whether true or not, fires on the mountain were reassuring.

The wagon road, which was opened in 1848, was the shortest and best road westward across the eastern crest of the Sierra Nevada. It was, nevertheless, a very difficult road. Seven years after its opening, George Goddard, commissioned to survey the approaches to Carson Valley for California, came down Carson (Woodford's) Canyon. His description of it is vivid!

"It was quite dusk when we arrived at the head of the famed Carson Canyon, and we had not proceeded far before the overhanging cliffs and dark pines above our heads, involved us in total obscurity. The roughness of the road, too, warned us that we had no easy task before us, in getting down this mountain chasm in the dark. Neither of us had traveled over this road before, so we had to trust pretty much to the mules, whose instinct generally keeps them right. We spent three of the longest hours in blundering down this place in the dark, and when at last we did emerge, the light of the stars was even dazzling to the eyes, so totally and painfully obscure had it been. A good supper, however, at Cary's, soon set us to rights again."

During the following ten years travelers west had to unhitch oxen, mules or horses at steep declivities, take the wheels from the wagons and use them as pulleys to hoist the wagon beds to the next highest level. For many years thereafter the broken parts of wagons lay along the sides of the canyon road, mute reminders of the once mighty exertions of man and beast in traveling this road.

The Washoe Indians

THE WASHOE INDIANS seen today on the streets of the towns and hamlets along the Carson. River and in the "colonies" at Dresslerville, Carson City and Reno, are descendants of a very ancient and a very primitive people. Before Bigler (1848), Goddard (1855) and DeGroot (c.1860) saw them and before their land was opened up to transcontinental travel, these Indians had lived undisturbed by other peoples for milleniums.

We may wonder what such men looked like, how they acted and what they thought in the early years of this intrusion. Both George Goddard and Henry DeGroot give us glimpses of them as they were when first encountered by the mining and homesteading Caucasians. DeGroot describes an encampment he encountered on the upper reaches of the East Fork of the Carson River in a pleasant little valley: "They have thus far been enabled to adhere to their customs and pursue their native modes of life in peaceful seclusion." Goddard, apparently encountering the same encampment five years earlier, observed that "since the days of Fremont (1844) they appear to have been uniformly friendly to the Whites." He continues that "they bear a high reputation for honesty amongst the inhabitants of Carson Valley."

In contrast to these views of primitive man uncontaminated is the lively account of another explorer, A.B. Powers, who, in the fall of 1855, led a party in the area near the distant Reynolds and Raymond Peaks on the headwaters of the Carson and far to the south of Carson Valley. Here they came unexpectedly upon ten or twelve Indian women, usually called squaws, clad in rabbit skins and digging, piling and roasting wild onions. Hidden nearby in a clump of quaking aspen were about twenty braves armed with bows and arrows, the escorts of these Stone-Age matrons, who came forward at the call of an old man. This man was a boss called Pah-sook, clothed in a blue flannel shirt and white fur hat draped with a black weed, for all the world like a misplaced "Broadway Swell," so his account goes! The braves called out, "How do you do!" The explorers calmed the fears of the Indians and there ensued conversation in the lingo of the emigrant trail that is Pike County, Missouri, English. These Indians were Washoes from Carson Valley out on a foraging expedition for food to be stored for winter use.

Reynolds Peak as seen from the south, near Ebbet's Pass. In 1855, this was a foraging area of the Washoe Indians. *(Courtesy of Juanita Schubert)*

Job's Peak

JOB'S PEAK has an elevation of 10,633 feet. Its lofty eminence was described in 1860 by Henry DeGroot, an early observer of its solid grandeur, as a partially "isolated, naked cone of bleached granite so white that at a distance it is apt to be taken for snow." The peak gets its name from the fact that Moses Job scaled its height in 1855 to plant the American flag on its very top. At its foot, situated where the hamlet of Sheridan grew up, was his store called, appropriately, "Job's." In 1855, this store was described by George H. Goddard during his survey of an immigrant wagon road and the eastern boundary of the state of California, as "the principal store in the valley."

It was at Job's where the replacement supplies were purchased after a nocturnal disaster on the emigrant trail. The mules in Goddard's pack train were frightened at the ghostly shadows of cattle moving slowly among the sage bushes and stampeded, scattering the contents of the pack containing the provisions. In the darkness, it took more than an hour to recover the groceries from along the road. The coffee, shot, and candles were never found. Job's store provided the "rescue" goods.

Of Job's Peak Henry DeGroot, writing in 1860, said: "It stands a partially isolated, naked cone of bleached granite, so white that at a distance it is apt to be taken for snow. It has no vegetation and but little timber upon it."

Frustration, on Coming to the Sierra Nevada Range from the East

T HE SIERRA Nevada Range as seen from Carson Valley has been likened by travelers to other of the world's lofty snow-capped and cloud-enveloped ranges — the Alps, and even the T'ien Shan, the "heavenly mountains" of China's western frontier lands. One viewer says: "To the south and immediately west, towering grandly to great height rise the majestic peaks of the Sierra Ne-

vada . . ." But to many — nay, to most — of those who approached these inspiring heights from the east, they were a barrier between them and the realization of their dreams of wealth to be won in the Eldorado of the West. And, in later years, to others who found it impossible to go beyond them to the civilization and culture of California, they were a hateful, frustrating obstacle.

What passions these mountains could raise in the early Fifties in the minds of immigrants to the Golden State may be envisioned from the account of Abner Blackburn, scribe of the company that settled for a few months at their base in 1850. Here the young men who had brought their goods all the long way across the plains and deserts between the Missouri and the Carson found that their wagons must be abandoned and that they had to pack over the mountains. Blackburn says that the boys would go on a spree in which they cut up harness, bent guns around trees, ran a lot of wagons together and set them afire, and ran amuck generally.

The lofty Sierra Nevada barrier. *(Courtesy of Juanita Schubert)*

The Paradise of Quadrapeds

O N SEPTEMBER 3, 1850, John Wood (whose boyhood home was Chilicothe, Ohio) and several companions abandoned their wagons at Rag Town, killed their last steer and with their blankets strapped on their backs, "every man for himself," started on foot along the Carson River to reach the distant mountains. He estimated their snowy summits to be 16,000 feet high! These were the Sierra Nevada Mountains, from which a beautiful small stream of pure cold water flowed.

Early on September 8, sore-footed, his boots having rubbed the skin off, Wood and his companions reached "Carson's Valley," which he said "is beautiful and afforded great grass tall enough to mow." Here the weary walker found thousands of mules, horses and cattle being rested, recuperating from their life-destroying trek down the Humboldt and across the Forty-Mile Desert to reach at long last this "paradise of quadrapeds."

But it was far from being a paradise of men. It was every man for himself! Trading posts were everywhere with hundreds of hungry men begging their way from one to another. Wood's feet were so sore he could barely walk. He was hobbling painfully to a trading post to get some flour when an "angel in disguise" asked him if he would like to ride a good horse over the mountains. The "angel," Mr. McClelen, on the next morning led his cattle out of "paradise", with the aid of the suffering but now mounted Wood, into the land of promise — California!

The paradise of quadrapeds. *(Courtesy of James Lawrence)*

6

Alta California Telegraph Company,

HAVING OFFICES AT

Santa Clara,
San Jose,
San Leandro,
Martinez,

Benicia,
Vallejo,
Napa,
Suisun,

Sacramento,
El Dorado,
Diamond Springs,
Placerville,

Coloma,
Auburn,
Grass Valley,
Nevada,

San Juan,
Camptonville,
Forest City,
Downieville,

Iowa Hill,
Yankee Jims,
Todd's Valley,
Georgetown,

Volcano,
Jackson,
Mokelumne Hill,
San Andreas,

Murphy's,
Columbia,
Sonora,
Folsom,

Connecting with YREKA, SHASTA, MARYSVILLE, AND CARSON VALLEY LINES.

OFFICE, NO. 153 MONTGOMERY STREET, CORNER OF MERCHANT.

OPEN FROM 8, A. M. TO 9 P. M. SUNDAYS, 9 TO 11, A. M.

[handwritten message:]

Yreka Dec 13 1859

To August Dougherty

Telegraph to F. Manlebaury,
Sacramento, and inform him
that you have arrived

F Dougherty

Markt & Co

TELEGRAPHIC

PLACERVILLE AND ST. JOSEPH
OVERLAND TELEGRAPH CO,

Offices at Genoa and Carson City, in Western Utah, connecting with all the
California Lines at Placerville.

Dispatches forwarded promptly to Camp Floyd, Salt Lake City and all points throughout the Territory of Nevada.

Towne & Bacon, Printers, San Francisco.

San Francisco Dec 12 1859.

To P F Dangberg

Arrived today — Will
you meet us here — Answer immedly
by telegraph

August Danberg

6 o'clock, ___ minutes, P M.

Mr. and Mrs. Frederick William Stodieck, one of the first German couples to settle in Carson Valley. Mr. Stodieck came from Halle in Westphalia in 1864. He returned to Germany in 1868 to claim his bride, Catherine Schulte. *(Courtesy of Lois Stodieck Jones)*

Winter

DECEMBER OF 1859 was a month of bitter cold and heavy storms in Carson Valley. It began snowing ten days before the first day of the month and it was still snowing on the tenth. During the summer when he had seen the heavy grazing of vast numbers of livestock along the grassy banks of the river, "Tennessee," correspondent of the *San Francisco Herald,* had prophesied great suffering if there came a heavy winter. It came! With lack of feed, intense cold, carcasses everywhere, hooves frozen off, the paradise of quadrapeds was turned into a graveyard.

On December 10, a man froze to death in Woodfords one hour after alighting from his horse. Thirty or forty men were stranded in the town of Genoa, sleeping in hay lofts over livery stables. The suffering of man and beast made doleful copy. Three days after Christmas, the correspondent himself felt the pinch: there was no turkey, no eggs, little milk and the whiskey was poor. The misery continued into the next year. The town was full of sick men living off the innkeepers; quarrels were frequent. At length on February 11, five men were "prostrated from the effects of pistol shots!"

Into this inhospitable world there came on the evening of December 24 a young German couple from their home in the village of Halle in Westphalia, a province of Prussia. They were Heinrich August Dangberg, a younger brother of H.F. Dangberg who had settled on the East Fork of the Carson River two years earlier, and his bride Frederika. The young couple had left in September in ample time to avoid arrival in Carson Valley in winter. It was known in far away Halle that crossing the Sierra Nevada in winter was difficult and dangerous.

August and Frederika came by way of Panama. Heavy storms on the Atlantic delayed their arrival in New York and, hence, on the west coast. Nevertheless, they arrived safely in Woodfords on Christmas Eve. How, one may ask, could this have been accomplished without snow plows? The answer is that it was done by the use of horses shod with horse snow shoes and a mighty faith in destiny as represented by the new world.

We have a description of these shoes which were fastened on the hooves of horses trailing one after the other. The shoes were made of a block of wood an inch thick and eight inches square, with a light plate of steel on top, canvas on the bottom, and holes in the steel plate for the caulks of the horse's shoes to go through. A band came over the hooves with a thumb screw to fasten down tight. This homely contraption enabled the young German couple to complete the last leg of their journey.

7

Settlement

TWO YEARS after the Carson River Route was opened up by Henry Bigler in 1848, H. S. Beatie and Abner Blackburn set up a temporary trading post at a site known later as Old Mormon Station. On June 1, 1851, Colonel John Reese established a permanent settlement a mile south of Beatie at a site selected by his nephew Stephen A. Kinsey. This was also known as Mormon Station and was re-named Genoa in 1855. Six weeks after Reese, on July 14, 1851, young Israel Mott and his wife arrived in Carson Valley with a California-bound emigrant train. Mott decided to remain in the valley at a place on the Carson River Route four miles south of Reese. Here he built a house for his wife out of abandoned wagon beds.

With the exception of Mott's, the first settlements in Carson Valley were made by groups of men frequently calling themselves companies. What were these companies? Not, it is clear, the associations "organized and existing" under the laws of a state or territory with which we are now familiar. They were, instead, groups of men pooling their resources — animals, wagons, gear, grain, gold dust — for a specific purpose. Why was this done? The men themselves were individualists of the first order, independent adventurers. Why did they want to limit themselves by associating with anyone? They were in a country without government, without law and order. One answer is that an individual in a totally free land is peculiarly vulnerable.

This is a fact recognized in legend and tradition the world over. Those ancient Greek heroes, Castor and Pollux, ventured into unknown lands as a pair, not as individuals.

Like them are the Weasel brothers of the Washoe tales, who, on their travels, aided and abetted each other in all sorts of exploits. In Carson Valley the proliferation of this type of association is illustrated by the linking of such familiar pioneer names as Woodward and Chorpenning who contracted with the United States as A. Woodward and Company to carry the mail; Chorpenning and Holliday who succeeded to the contract when Woodward was killed; Mandelbaum and Klauber, Salmon and Johnson who were merchants; Dangberg and Mast, and Adams and Brown who were ranchers; Kingsbury and McDonald, who were toll road builders, and others.

How the necessity for having a partner or forming a company was impressed on one of these men is illustrated by the experience of H.F. Dangberg who took up a claim in Carson Valley in 1856. On one occasion when he left his claim either to purchase supplies or to sell his produce — beef or butter — he returned to find Lucky Bill Thorington seated on the step of his cabin with a gun across his knees. Lucky Bill was indulging in a practice known as claim jumping which had been reported in Carson Valley in the previous summer *(San Francisco Herald,* July 6, 1855). The charming gambler, who also enjoyed the reputation of being a frontier Robin Hood, was smiling when Dangberg rode up. With his hand on the trigger he said, "What are you going to do now, Dutchman?"

Dangberg said not a word but, vowing in his heart to recover his claim under more favorable circumstances, turned his horse and rode away. Early in the following year he went above Thorington on the East Fork of the Carson River where he staked out another claim. In this instance Dangberg was a partner in a company with Charles Holbrook and Ben Mast. Forty-seven years later, in 1902, Dangberg recovered his first claim, which was by then known as the Klauber Ranch.

The artist conveys in this pen and ink sketch of the first permanent house built in 1851 by Colonel Reese something of the unutterable loneliness that descended on the men, women and children who elected to tarry at the foot of the eastern slope of the Sierra Nevada. *(Courtesy of James A. Lawrence)*

Eastfork Carson River, November 6th 1857

Compagnie account betwin Benjamen G.
Mast — Charles C. Holbrock and H.F. Dangberg

Put in the Compagnie by B. Mast and F. Dangberg.

Nov 6	2 Doz Milk Pans bot of Klauson	$ 17. 44
"	" 3 Milk Sives and 1 Schourn	2,50
"	" 10 lbs Nails bot of Han	1,50
"	" 1 Grind stone bot of Sisk	2,00
"	" 100 lbs New orleans Sugar at 16 $	26,00
"	" 35 lbs Coffee at 22 $	7,70
"	" 50 lbs fine Salt at 10 $	5,00
"	" 1 Sack No 2 Schot	5,25
"	" Trumphireous of Sloans	43,00
"	" 5 Ga Syrup at $2 pr	11,00
"	" 12 lb Steel at 22 $	2,75
"	" 6 Cans Powder at 70 cts	4,20
"	" 2 Oxen	400
"	" 2 Oxbandes	1,00
"	" 1 Syth & Snath	2,50
"	" 1 Knife at 1 Fork	2,00
"	" 2 Sack of Turnips	78,00
"	" 1 Waggon	55,00
Dec 16	57 lbs of Beef at 12½ cts	7,12½

Put in the Compagnie by Charles Holbrock

Nov 6	3000 lbs Wheat	$ 90,00
"	" 300 lbs of Wheat	10,00
"	" 2 Hogs	36,00
"	" 140 lbs of Flour	5,80

Dangberg, Mast and Holbrook formed a partnership (compagnie) in 1857. Some of the items that were the basis of this business venture are transcribed as follows:

East fork Carsson Rever November the 6th, 1857 Compagnie account betwin Benjamen G. Mast, Charles C. Holbrook and H. F. Dangberg

Put in the compagnie by B. Mast and F. Dangberg

Nov. 6 2 Doz. Milk Pans bot of Nisson	$17.00
,, ,, 10 lbs Nails bot of Van (Henry Van Sickle)	1.50
,, ,, 100 lbs New orleans Shugar at 26 cts	26.00
,, ,, 35 lbs Coffee at 22c	7.70
,, ,, 2 sets of Harniss	78.00
,, ,, 1 waggon	55.00

Put in the Compagnie by Charles Holbrook

Nov. 6 3000 lbs Wheat	$20.00
,, ,, 2 Hoggs	30.00

Another page from the Account Book of H. F. Dangberg tells how the pioneers traded with one another. Some of these trades are described in the following transcription:

East Fork Carsson Rever Oct the 15th 1858

Trading Account for the Compagnie of B. Mast & H. F. Dangberg

Oct. 15 Sold two Hoggs weight 252 lbs at 12 cts	
Oct. 15 Bought 312 lbs of Flour at 10 cts of D. Jones	
Oct. 22 Received of Winters on Potatos 11,12 lbs at 2 cts	
Oct. 22 Agreed to pay for bringing of the Potatos $1.50 cts	
0Nov. 29 loaned to Klauber in Casch	$100.00
Dec. 16 paid for the Work Oxen to Winters	$165.00
Dec. 16 paid to A. Montgomry for balanc on a	
Dec. 16 Trade betwin Flour and a Horss	$20.00
March 3 Sold to Vansickel (P. W. Van Sickel)	
March 3 the old Spannoich Cow for	45.00
March 10 pd to James Maddisson for 1 Months Work	35 Dollars

GENOA - NEVADA'S FIRST TOWN

Genoa — Settled in 1851

I N HIS *Men to Match My Mountains,* Irving Stone remarks that in the old west "what happens in one region is of tremendous consequence to the others." This observation, made of the vast area of western America *before* it was cut up into artificial units — states, counties, and townships where man-made boundaries have limited historians to writing about arbitrary units of reality — is universally true. In no way can this be better illustrated than by the history of Genoa, the town that was originally called Mormon Station.

Genoa, where the first permanent house in Nevada was built by Colonel John Reese in 1851, is situated about one mile south of the Old Mormon Station which was a roofless log cabin built by H.S. Beatie in 1850. Genoa was given its name by Elder Orson Hyde of Salt Lake City who,

in 1855, became the first Probate Judge in western Utah when Nevada was Carson County, Utah Territory. Hyde made a plan of the town which would have insured its orderly development. However, "the best made plans of mice and men go aft a'gley" and, in this case, the role of fate was played by Brigham Young who, on September 15, 1857, ordered the Mormon settlers in western Utah back to Zion. By November 20, men reported that in Genoa business was dull; no one had any money

There was a recovery, however, in 1858. On December 18 of that year, Alfred James and W.L. Jernegan of Placerville moved into town to start a weekly paper called the *Territorial Enterprise.* No sooner were they set up for business in the Nevada Hotel than the storms set in which kept the town in comparative isolation until the following May. Supplies of all kinds grew scarce. Snowshoe Thompson and others packed paper in for the *Territorial Enterprise;* speculators cornered the market for provisions — flour went to $25 per barrel and bacon to 50 cents a pound. Spring storms made the situation even worse. In late May, Captain Jim of the Washoe tribe had 25 of his braves on snowshoes packing supplies from Strawberry

Genoa's Main Street about 1874 when the trustee's map was made. The first building on the left is the Raycraft Livery Stable. The last building is the court house. (*Courtesy of Josephine Raycraft Hellwinkel*)

Log cabin — Genoa. Left to right: John Titus, Henry Walker, Frank Walker, W.R. Adams, Del Williams, Jack Raycraft, Dr. Luce, Walter Gelatt, Dr. Young, Robert Falcke, Bill Frey, Knute, Ray Dake, Bill Parsons, Drummer, Leo Hawkins, True Van Sickle, George Van Sickle, Bill Murphy, Frank Smith, Bill Fulton and Noah Blossom.

Genoa's main street before 1910. Looking south and to the left from the Odd Fellows Hall with the Harris Store on the first floor (until 1895) are cabins, then the Central Hotel, Hansen's Saloon (the Metropolitan Saloon in 1862) and Gilman's Hotel (the Nevada Hotel in 1862), standing at the corner of Nixon and Main streets. All these buildings burned in the fire of 1910. *(Courtesy of Lena Gardelli Falcke)*

Approaching Genoa, which according to J. Wells Kelly writing in 1862, "is pleasantly situated on the west side of the Carson River about half way down the valley. On the south a high bald mountain, projecting like a huge bastion from the main range, shelters it from strong winds and severe storms that mostly come from that quarter, while on the west and immediately over it, the mighty Sierra dark with woods and cut with deep ravines, lifts itself to the height of several thousand feet. Spread out before it to the east are the rich meadows and pastures of Carson Valley with the willow-fringed river winding through it. The landscape in front is as beautiful as can be conceived — the scenery behind bold and majestically grand." *(Courtesy of Nevada Department of Highways)*

over the Johnson Cut-off (now Echo Summit) road to Genoa. The winter finally broke and the monopoly too when, on June 28, Abraham Klauber arrived with twenty wagonloads of supplies which brought about a reduction in prices ranging from 50 to 75 per cent.

Mr. Klauber, whose business acumen may be recognized by his appearance in Genoa at this critical moment, was an immigrant from Bohemia who engaged in various successful business ventures in California and Nevada in these early years. He built his house, which he used as his store, in 1859. The frame building stood just north of the site where later a store was built. There was added to this, after 1868, a second story which was the Odd Fellows Hall. The stone basement of this Klauber structure may still be seen west and south of the court house (Museum). Soon Mr. Klauber had three clerks working for him; his merchandising practices continued to be praised by the people of Genoa and played no small part in the rising fortunes of the town.

Genoa flourished between 1860 and 1869. Many a night during these years of heavy hauling between California and Virginia City, the main street of the town was so packed with freight wagons and teams that horses, mules and oxen were tied to the wheels of their wagons to feed overnight because stable room was not available. In these years it was almost impossible for a pedestrian to walk the street without the risk of getting his head kicked off, as Judge Virgin once related to Bert Selkirk, editor, in 1904, of the *Record Courier*.

Genoa was the child of roads, and roads brought her to an early decline. The first inkling of her future doom was the opening of the King's Canyon Toll Road in 1863, making Carson City her initial rival on a shorter route between Virginia City and Placerville.

Two years earlier, a north-south road, by-passing Genoa, had been opened up when the Cradlebaugh toll bridge was built across the Carson River. It shortened by eight miles the distance between Carson City and the Twelve Mile House, a station situated at the southern end of Carson Valley on the "Road to Esmeralda" and the mines of

Aurora to the south.

A more remote rival than Carson City but a more deadly one, as the wheel of fortune turned, was the town of Reno on the trans-continental railroad built by the Central Pacific. When the railroad was completed in 1869, it immediately became the shortest and fastest "road" by all counts between the eastern seaboard and the Pacific coast.

Some idea of the severity of the shock administered to the flourishing frontier town of Genoa in 1869 may be envisioned by a count of the exchanges of property which took place along the Carson River Route immediately following that fateful year. From deeds recorded in Douglas County it appears that an average of something over a hundred exchanges took place each year after 1863. This number jumped to 199 in 1870, 259 in 1871, and 261 in 1872. The shock is further demonstrated by the fact that only 15 exchanges of property are recorded for the following seven years.

The diary of John McQuig, who passed through Genoa in 1869, bears contemporary witness to the decline. He says, in contrast to earlier diarists who emphasized the activity of traders and travelers, that "Genoa was apparently supported by farmers in the valley and the little travel by stage across the mountains on the Placerville and Big Tree routes." The latter served the mining communities of Alpine County, California. In 1869, these camps, so blithely called "cities" by their founders of a few years earlier, were also in decline.

Genoa, however, again recovered. From 1869 on for a number of years, Nevada's first town was the chief stopping place for the north-south stage lines and a shopping center for the ranchers of Carson Valley. She received a fresh impetus toward revival in the late 1870's when Bodie was booming and all roads leading southward were bearing heavy traffic. This was, however, a short-lived period of prosperity. At the same time a new road in Carson Valley connected Gilman's settlement on the East Fork of the Carson (which became Gardnerville) with the Twelve Mile House. Thus hay and grain grown on the neighboring ranches passed directly on to the road to Bodie.

One after another new roads and new settlements eroded the early basis of Genoa's pre-eminence. In 1895, C.P. Young, Noah Blossom and the Harris family, long successful and prosperous merchants in Genoa, saw the handwriting on the wall. The first two closed their stores. Mrs. Harris and her stepson Abe decided to move one of their buildings and their store to the new town of Gardnerville.

An eyewitness viewed the moving, an act that must have shaken the faith of even Judge Virgin in the viability of the old town as much as it delighted the teen-aged Bert Selkirk, who describes the momentous undertaking. The building was a small dwelling that stood north of the Central Hotel. It was loaded on two twelve-by-twelve-foot skids shod with steel, the front end resting on the front wheels

The Reese cabin and stockade in 1869, drawing by L. L. Hawkins. *(Courtesy of Clifford Barret)*

of an old logging wagon. Then twenty-four horses were hitched to this unwieldy assembly and when the driver gave the signal to start they were off down the hill — not at a good pace — the first heave took them only a few feet. At long last, however, the horses pulled the house down to the first bridge over the Carson River. There they stopped, unable to move farther. Men took over and decided to cut the building in two. When they finished sawing through the walls and timbers, and when providence provided a light snowfall, eight horses walked off to Gardnerville with half of the building!

The departure of the merchants was followed by the closing of the blacksmith shops. The sounds coming from the anvils, the odor of burning hooves, the clatter of wagons, the neighing of horses all but ceased. Genoa was left with only one reason for being: the transaction of county busi-

"That Rascal Pat!"

A Side Spliting Farce in One Act,

To be Given by

The Genoa Literary Society,

At Raycraft's Hall, Genoa,

Friday Evening, February 24, 1899.

———— ⋙⋘ ————

CAST OF CHARACTERS:

Pat McNoggerty, a handy servant..........................Ray Dake.

Major Puffjacket, on half pay.................................A. L. Rice.

Chas. Livingston, poor but ambitious..............Frank Smith.

Laura, Puffjacket's niece, **In Love with Charles,** Mabel Ritchford.

Nancy, her maid, in Love with Pat................Edna Tillman.

A Splendid Entertainment,

To be followed by a

SOCIAL DANCE!

The Proceeds of the Entertainment will be given to the Rev. J. Johns.

Admission, 25 cts.; — — — children under 12 yrs., free

(Courtesy Nevada State Park Commission)

ness at the brick courthouse. The recording of deeds and mortgages, operating the county jail, and holding district court sustained the old town until 1916. In that year, H.F. Dangberg, Jr., implementing a need originally envisioned by pioneer Genoa resident, Lawrence Gilman, led the citizens of the center of the valley in a drive to remove the county seat to the heart of the agricultural and stock-raising community of Carson Valley. This was accomplished by an act of the legislature with the support of widely circulated petitions. The ten-year-old town of Minden was chosen as the new county seat.

In 1934, the coming of Nevada cartoonist Lewis Hymers (his wife had grown up in Genoa where her father, Hans Jepsen, was county clerk and treasurer from 1900 to 1922) signaled a revival of interest in the old frontier town. Hymers was followed in 1945 by Hans Meyer-Kassel, a distinguished European artist. Slowly others, led by the discerning eye of these latter-day pioneers, have been attracted by Genoa's unique qualities, the charm of its fragrant lilacs, its snowballs, its blossoming orchards in springtime and its golden Lombardy poplars in autumn. After passing through many phases of prosperity and decay, Genoa, the first and fairest town of Nevada as many would claim, has been reborn.

The Centennial — 1961

IN CELEBRATION of the Centennial of Nevada's first settlement, held at Genoa in 1951, a commemorative stamp was issued. The design for the stamp was taken from a painting by the distinguished German artist Hans Meyer-Kassel who became a resident of Genoa in 1945. The painting is now owned by former Governor of Nevada, Charles Russell. The stamp (the initial order was for 110,000,000) was chosen by the California Collectors Club of San Francisco as "The Most Attractive Stamp issued in 1951" and as "The Best Designed" stamp of 1951 by the readers of *Linn's Weekly Stamp News*.

Hans Meyer was born in Kassel, Germany, on March 8, 1872. His preparatory education was received in his birthplace followed by enrollment at the University of Leipsig. He studied for a number of years at the Academy of Art in Munich.

As a member of the International Art Society of Munich, two signal honors were accorded him in recognition of his

(Courtesy of Maria Meyer-Kassel)

14

Clara Frank and two young Washoes in gala attire for the Centennial. (© *James A. Lawrence*)

outstanding talent: his native city acclaimed him by adding the word Kassel to his name and the Emperor of Germany, through the Royal Ministry of Education, bestowed on him the title of Professor.

In 1922, Professor Meyer-Kassel and his wife moved to the United States where he maintained a studio in New York City for the next ten years. Here he was recognized as a master of portraiture. He came to Nevada in 1936. In 1940, he received the Honorary Medal issued by I.B.M. (International Business Machines) through its Gallery of Science and Art "for notable contributions to the art of the world."

Painting was his life and his brush was never idle. On the afternoon of August 29, 1952, after completing a portrait, he laid down his palette and brushes for a few hours rest — a rest that became eternal during the early hours of August 30, 1952.

His widow, Maria Meyer-Kassel, has a collection of these fine impressionistic paintings which well illustrate his noted versatility.

The Adams House

PERSONS BEARING the names of distinguished families have, from time to time, come to Carson Valley. Probably the earliest of these were John Quincy Adams and his brother Rufus, originally from Adams County, Illinois. They emigrated first to Utah Territory and finally, in 1853, to Carson Valley. The brothers settled one mile north of Genoa where they engaged in ranching and brickmaking. After selling one half of the ranch in 1853, they built, before 1864, the handsome brick residence where the heirs of John Quincy Adams still live.

For five years the house was a hotel on the Carson River Route. It was called the Adams House. The steps which now lead to the three doors seen behind the stately columns originally extended around both ends of the house.

The Adams house about 1940. *(Courtesy of James A. Lawrence)*

Mr. and Mrs. John Q. Adams. *(Courtesy of Nevada State Park Commission)*

The door on the north end led to the bar, the center door to a hall leading back to the dining room and the south door to the parlor and family living quarters. Access to the second story was originally by an outside stairway on the north of the house. Here on the second floor were bedrooms for hotel guests and a spacious ballroom!

A party on the emigrant trail? Yes, indeed there were many of them as echoes from the walls of the Adams ballroom would confirm. Perhaps the ladies were not always from Pike County, Missouri, clad in red calico skirts and bodices; perhaps their escorts did not always wear hickory shirts, as one correspondent of a California newspaper implies. In fact, the Adams House was the proper setting for silk gowns and white shirts. The account books of early settlers in Carson Valley often included, in lists of clothing bought, at least a couple of white shirts!

The Genoa Court House

L AW AND ORDER on the Carson River Route suffered from many ills and incongruities — judges threatened by contending parties, grand juries that declined to indict proven thieves, court rooms improvised in barns. Genoa's first court house was typical. It was acquired by the local government in 1859 from the Catholic church. In contemporary accounts, it is described as an old building being repaired, thirty by sixty feet, one and one-half stories high with clapboards in front and rough boards stood up endwise on the sides. It had shakes for a roof and when replaced with the present structure was used as a livery stable. The amount of $750 had been allowed to put it in shape. In spite of this expenditure, Judge John Cradlebaugh had to hold his first session of court in the loft, access to which was by a ladder from the street. Artist Lew Hymers caught the humor of this situation.

The fine court house which replaced it in 1865 was made from brick fired in the kilns of the Adams brothers situated near the Old Mormon Station. It was constructed by Rufus Adams and Lawrence Gilman.

Let it not be thought, however, that only the solemnities of government brought the pioneers to the Court House, as witness the description of a ball in the *Carson Valley News* for Saturday, February 16, 1875.

The ball was given by the local chapter, or grange, of the nationwide organization founded in 1867 as the National Grange (*Farm*) or *Patrons of Industry*. At the time the ball was given this organization, to further the interests of farmers and agriculture, had granges in all of the states of the Union and a membership of 1,500,000. The account which follows, condensed from the original, bears some marks of promotional enthusiasm on the part of the editor of the newspaper, A.C. Pratt:

"The Ball, or Calico Party, as the invitation committee termed it in their circulars, took place on Wednesday evening of this week, at the Court House. This was the first

Cartoon by Lew Hymers.

The White House (known in 1858 as the Gilbert Hotel) was purchased by the Rice Brothers in 1872. It stood on Main Street opposite the court house until after 1910. *(Courtesy of the Nevada State Historical Society)*

Genoa's new courthouse. *(Courtesy Nevada State Highway Dept.)*

The Genoa court house. *(Courtesy of Juanita Jarvis Malo)*

public entertainment given by the Carson Valley Grange, No. 3, and was one of the largest, respectable and agreeable gatherings that it has ever been our good fortune to attend, exceeding the anticipations of the most sanguine Granger in the county, and proving a success such as to gratify the members of the Order, and fill the breasts of both sexes with pride at the happy termination of their initial general public assemblage. It may safely be said that no previous terpsichorean party given in Douglas can claim to have excelled this in any of the elements that go to make up a highly enjoyable and in every particular satisfactory display. The hundred and fifty ladies and gentlemen, masters and misses Wednesday night who came together for social communion with one another and to mingle together in the mazy and inspiriting dance was a sight pleasurable to behold. Every greeting of sometime separated friends and acquaintances, every gleam of the eye of the great collection of brave men and lovely women denoted to the looker-on how great were the emotions of enjoyment prevailing.

"As a matter of course, this being a 'Calico Party', there was no attempt by any of the attendants at elaboration or elegance of dress. It would have been unfitting for the wives and daughters and sons of our farmers to have perked themselves up in gaudy finery and deceitful gems . . . and it was the general remark how lovely is woman unadorned. . . . Woman's true charm and man's noble bearing were exhibited in their true light . . . everyone moved with natural and unrestrained ease and grace. No impediments

of dress stood in the way of the most complete and free participation in the pleasures of the occasion . . .

"Under the leadership and direction of Mr. C.M. Taylor, the musicians seemed to outdo themselves, vieing with each other in delicacy of execution and artistic performance, swelling into the most bewildering strains of harmonious and intoxicating melody, and captivating the senses by a flood of charming sounds, and melting the soul in a volume of sweet vibrations, falling upon the ear with ravishing cadences, and nerving the weary dancers to unflagging graces of motion to the last . . .

"At midnight the party adjourned for supper. This consisted of a bountiful quantity of excellent and well-prepared viands contributed by individual Grangers, and spread in the large dining hall of the White House. The Messrs. Rice arranged the table with exquisite taste, the surrounding cleanliness imparting a zest of appetite in the guests that resulted in full and eager justice being done to the various choice delicacies and substantials.

". . . It was universally voted that this was one of the most pleasant and unique and *recherche* parties ever given in Genoa. And Carson Valley Grange can justly pride itself upon having gotten up and carried to great success a grand and unsurpassed evening's entertainment. It may be taken for granted," Mr. Pratt concluded, "that this flourishing Order will inaugurate periodical reunions of this handsome character."

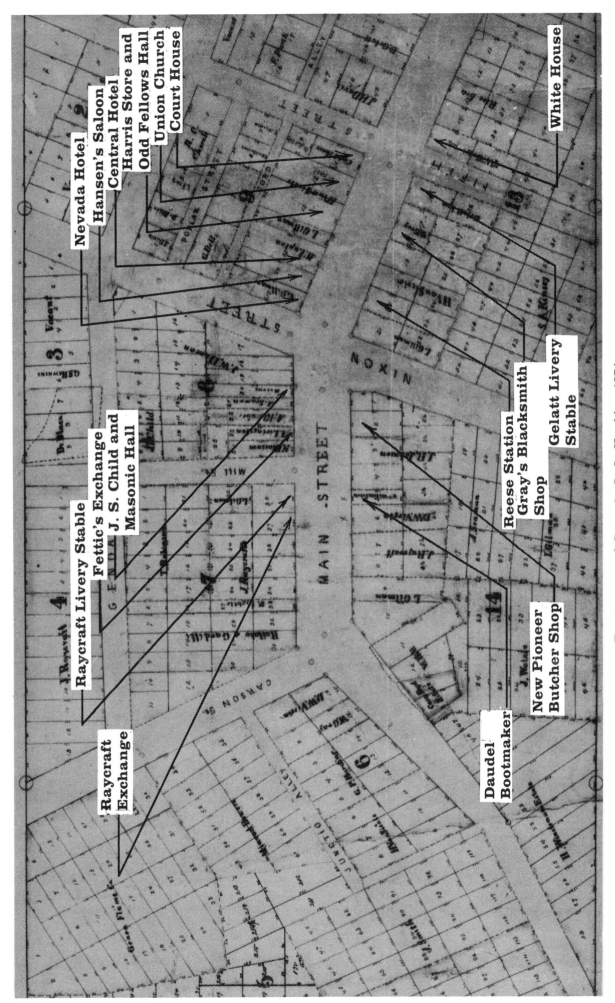

Nevada Hotel
Hansen's Saloon
Central Hotel
Harris Store and
Odd Fellows Hall
Union Church
Court House

White House

Raycraft Livery Stable
Fettic's Exchange
J. S. Child and
Masonic Hall

Reese Station
Gray's Blacksmith
Shop
Gelatt Livery
Stable

Raycraft
Exchange

Daudel
Bootmaker

New Pioneer
Butcher Shop

Trustees map of Genoa by L. L. Hawkins, 1874.

21

The Harris Store

MR. M. HARRIS founded his Genoa store about 1875, occupying for this purpose the lower stories of the Masonic and Odd Fellows halls, the latter being a part of the old Klauber buildings. The advertising and merchandising techniques of the Harris family never seem to have faltered. In the years of his life in Carson Valley, Mr. Harris never ceased to seek advantages in trade. When the "boom" began in Bodie, he turned his store over to the management of his clerks and took to the road with a peddler's wagon. On his return from one of these trips to the mining camps, he found his store in the hands of a receiver, his judgment of his clerks in grave error. After bankruptcy proceedings his wife, Mrs. Annie M. Harris, asserted her prerogatives and in 1891 had herself declared a "trader sole," reputedly the first woman granted this privilege in the state of Nevada.

Mrs. Harris opened her store on the first floor of the Odd Fellows building. It flourished and was soon the leading store in the community. One of the devices Mrs. Harris employed to make it so was to serve dinner to shoppers, wives of farmers and their children who came to Genoa every two or three months to purchase supplies for family and ranch. Often from fifteen to twenty guests sat around the Harris family table. The invitation was never related to the amount of goods bought.

Many are the tales of the kindness of this able woman, such as that of the ne'er-do-well whose credit was gone, whose child had died and had to be buried — a tale of woe indeed. Mrs. Harris gave him $60 for which he signed a note. Her judgment was right . . . he never repaid the loan!

Hansen's Saloon

T. N. (TIGE) HANSEN was an ex-woodsman, a native of Denmark, who in his early years had amassed a "fortune" in Alpine County. On coming to Genoa in 1886 he opened his saloon on the west side of Genoa's Main Street in what, in 1862, had been known as the Metropolitan Saloon. Here he enjoyed the patronage of former

Hansen's Saloon: Proprietor "Tige" Hansen behind the bar. (*Courtesy of Josephine Raycraft Hellwinkel*)

Fettic's Exchange, purchased by Frank Fettic in December of 1884. In 1862 it was known as Livingston's Exchange. *(Courtesy of James A. Lawrence)*

cronies all during the summer months when crews of men on the wood drive were floating logs and cord wood down the Carson River to be used by the inhabitants of Virginia and Carson cities.

On the eve of the Fourth of July, 1893, Bert Selkirk, a lad of fifteen years (he was born March 28, 1878) fresh from his home in Sacramento, was strolling northward along the boardwalk on the west side of Main Street when a shot was fired and a crowd gathered in front of Hansen's Saloon. Selkirk and his companion rushed forward to the porch of the saloon where a man, not identified, lay, his head in a pool of blood. Young Selkirk, after being informed that this was the custom in Genoa — a man was shot for breakfast each morning — was on the point of returning to the peace and quiet of Sacramento's cobblestone-paved streets when his friend's sister assured him that this breakfast food was served in the boom days in the mining town of Bodie, and was not a delicacy dished up in Genoa. Young Selkirk's nerves were steadied and he stayed to become, on November 11, 1904, the well-known editor and owner of the *Record Courier,* published every Friday in Gardnerville, Nevada. He remained as editor and publisher for forty years until October 1944.

Fettic's Exchange

FETTIC'S EXCHANGE was owned and operated in the last century by Frank Fettic, designated as the "grand old man" of those days. He came to Genoa in 1883 where he operated a "gentlemen's saloon," allowing no rough stuff and seldom, if ever, did he tolerate drinking to excess.

Frank Fettic was deeply interested in both politics and lodges. It was his habit to attend political conventions, and whenever he went out of town he hired a neighbor to mind the Exchange. On one such occasion, Charles Daudel, the little old German bootmaker whose shop was across the street, was pinch-hitting for Mr. Fettic when a group of men from the Diamond Sawmill in Alpine County rode into town. They found the mild little bootmaker in charge at Fettic's and thereupon decided to put on a show by riding their horses through the mullioned door into the bar and ordering drinks served them while mounted. Mr. Daudel at first refused to comply with their request. He was weakened in his stand, however, by the threat of bodily harm. Men and boys gathered outside the bar, peering in the windows at the exceptional sight, but ready to take to their heels en-masse when the raucous riders came back on the street.

Today this historic old bar is owned by Robert and Betty Carver who have a warning posted at the entrance stating *No Horses Allowed!*

Communications

IN THE SPRING of 1858, work was started on a telegraph line from Hangtown (Placerville) to Genoa and was completed in the fall. The first telegraph office was, according to local tradition, a humble edifice which was originally situated just south of the store of Mandelbaum and Klauber.

The coming of the telegraph is in perspective overshadowed by the arrival on December 18, 1858, of the founders of the *Territorial Enterprise* with their press and paper, ready to do business. They set up their works in the Nevada Hotel, the proprietor of which was Thomas J. Singleton. We quote from the first anniversary issue of the paper published in Carson City where the owners removed their enterprise on November 5, 1859:

"One year ago today, the first issue of the *Territorial Enterprise* was issued at Genoa. Our publishing room was in Singleton's hall, in the Nevada Hotel, a room indiscriminately used by preachers, debating clubs, secret societies, and once at least as a prison. Upon that occasion we had a man accused of crime chained to our printing press, with a chain, for two days and a half."

Puzzling to posterity is how the hall of the Nevada Hotel, the first home of the famous *Territorial Enterprise,* came in late years to be called the annex. To the solving of this and other mysteries of the old town, Arnold Trimmer, a resident of Genoa since 1909 when several of the early settlers were still living, has dedicated his leisure and his talents. With rare devotion to discovering the truth he has checked tradition against the records. It is Mr. Trimmer's conclusion that, when the new hotel was built in 1859 the

FRANK WALKER, A NATIVE OF GENOA, TOOK OFF ON SKIS FROM THE TOP OF THE MOUNTAIN BETWEEN VALLEY SPRINGS AND GENOA — TRAVELED SO FAST HIS SHIRT WAS TORN FROM HIS BACK! THIS SAME PIONEER CARRIED THE MAIL FROM GENOA TO MARKLEVILLE EVERY WINTER ON SKIS — SUCCESSFULLY MAKING THE GRADE EVEN WHEN LOADED WITH THE EARLY SPRING SHIPMENT OF MAIL ORDER CATALOGS

Cartoon by Lew Hymers.

hall was removed from the corner of Nixon and Main streets to the west end of Lot 24 in Block No. 8 on the north side of Mill Street, as shown on the trustee's map of 1874. It thus became the so-called annex or perhaps it was originally on its present site and was demoted to the status of an annex when the new hotel was built. In any case, the marks where the press was bolted to the floor of the hall were, until recently, to be seen on the parlor floor of the home of Mrs. Cerissa Mott Fettic who came into possession of the annex about 1889 and restored it to a status suitable to its historic past.

would instead take a sack of flour, a side of bacon and some beans and continue to draw on the balance until spring. When the spring work opened up on the ranches, the guns were redeemed.

On this occasion, the Washoe women, as we have said, decided that it would be better to be cold than hungry. They took their rabbit-skin blankets to Abe. He looked them over but his mother interfered before a deal could be made. The blankets were loaded with lice! Lest this remark cast an unduly unfavorable light on Washoe hygiene, it must be said that the blankets were usually deposited on ant hills in later spring where they were cleansed by the busy little insects before the next winter season.

Rabbit Skin Blankets

WINTERS IN Carson Valley although not too long were long enough for the Washoe tribesmen to enjoy their rabbit-skin blankets. However, the women of the tribe, in imitation of their menfolk, once tried to hock the blankets for food when spring was slow in coming. They got this idea from their husbands who year after year at the onset of winter brought their shotguns and rifles to the Harris store in Genoa where Abe, the stepson of the proprietress, would appraise them, attach a tag to each gun and give the owner credit for the value of the weapon. The Washoes never took the full amount at one time; they

Edna Coleman wearing a dress in the style of 1850 and still worn in 1950 by Washoe women. *(Courtesy of Anna Neddenriep Dressler)*

John Anthony and his wife Wama displaying rabbit skin blankets. *(Courtesy of Anna Neddenriep Dressler)*

Washoe Styles

IT WOULD BE wrong to impute a lack of adaptability to the Washoe Indians in the first half century of their contact with the intruding white people. They quickly acquired some of the outward manifestations of civilization, principally clothing. Both men and women soon got the idea that the human body should be concealed. They copied the calico dresses worn on the emigrant trail by the pioneer women and, until recently, this style has been perpetuated by them — a plain bodice and a full skirt which took approximately ten yards of calico. The men dressed like the men of the frontier. Until the present generation, the dictates of fashion never impressed them.

Occasionally they adopted modification of their dress aided by the vicissitudes of pioneer merchandising as the following accounts indicate. On one shipment of bolts of calico coming to the Harris store in Genoa from San Francisco, Mrs. Harris found, to her dismay, that Mr. Harris on his buying trip had selected cloth with startlingly loud black and gold stripes. This, the good lady decided, would be a total loss; no one would buy anything so gaudy. However, she had not reckoned with the taste of the Indian women. They bought up the entire bolt immediately and in a few hours had stitched themselves flashy gowns to delight their menfolk and themselves!

The Washoe men, as we have said, usually dressed in the everyday frontier style of their white brothers. On one occasion, however, the Harris merchandizing talent greatly modified this habit. When Mrs. Harris and stepson Abe were closing the Genoa store, preparatory to opening their store in Gardnerville, they discovered another mistake long concealed by Mr. Harris; namely, several trunks filled with Prince Albert coats. Again the Harris ingenuity saved the day with the aid of the Washoes. Abe got an Indian interested in this flamboyant, outmoded style and sold the entire stock to the Washoes for seven dollars per coat.

The Virgin House

THE CENTER portion of this gracious old house with its wide verandas, its peaked gables and wooden lace scrollwork trim originally stood on the land of Colonel John Reese on Mill Street and was in all probability built by Mart Gaige. It was moved to its present site, remodeled and enlarged by merchant J. R. Johnson of the Genoa firm of Salmon and Johnson mentioned in the *First Directory of Nevada Territory*. This he did prior to moving his family from the east to Genoa.

The moving of the house down Mill Street to its present site was viewed with skepticism by the citizens of the town. The successful accomplishment of this feat was looked upon as folly by the doubting Thomases of the community; this led Mr. Johnson to reassure them with a phrase that was forever after associated with his name: "Leave it to J.R., by gosh!"

In 1884, the house was purchased by Daniel Webster Virgin, a lawyer who came to Genoa in 1863 and remained there until his death in 1928 at the age of ninety-three. The verandas were added to the house by Judge Virgin's son-in-law, Louis Finnegan, some time after his marriage to the youngest daughter, Lillian, in 1904.

The judge was a man of many talents. He was, from 1889 to 1894, superintendent of schools in Douglas County, visiting each of the nine school districts at least twice a year. One of the pupils, Dave Park, reminiscing in 1962 at the age of 83 about the Judge addressing the pupils, said: "I remember his speaking and how well we could understand what he meant. It wasn't high-flowing language; he was clear, concise and to the point, and gave us a little counsel."

In further pursuit of his duties, the Judge wrote in his first report to State Superintendent Orvis Ring on the question of levying a special tax for school support, that the people would probably say "no" to such a tax. "But," he continued, "when the appeal was made to their generosity they were willing to give up to two or three times as much as their assessments would have amounted to, so I conclude that when you have school houses or churches to build and equip, the old-fashioned way of going about it beats the taxation method all hollow."

In addition to this position in the school system, the Judge served Douglas County both as judge and as district

The Virgin House, now known as the Pink House, was purchased in 1971 by Walter and Nora Merrell who offer cocktails, dining and dancing in the patio and rooms in the rear.

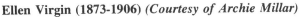

Ellen Virgin (1873-1906) *(Courtesy of Archie Millar)*

Lillian Virgin (1878-1939) was married to Louis Finnegan in 1904. In 1919, she founded the Candy Dance to raise funds for Genoa street lights. This dance has become a celebrated annual event. *(Courtesy of Archie Millar)*

attorney. Moreover, he had a flourishing law practice and many were the skeletons that came to rest in his files.

A visit to the Judge's home, graced by his wife and his gay and lovely daughters, was an event to be remembered. His wife, Mary Raycraft, was somewhat of a recluse but a famous cook, especially praised for her raspberry shortcake and home-made ice cream. Judge Virgin was an orchardist and he kept a cow which he milked each morning before clients came to his office and each evening after the last client had gone home. He also kept a horse. He had a long white beard; no one could remember that it had ever been dark. It was kept scrupulously clean, and those who knew him were often startled to hear form his lips a most unexpected and eloquent flow of frontier invective.

Self portrait of Henry and Edna Tillman in their home in Genoa about 1900. They are enjoying a family musical with father and mother Tillman and brother John looking down on them. *(Courtesy of Arthur Champagne)*

Stone bedroom of Warren Wasson (Indian agent 1859-1860, which stands in the barnyard of the Trimmer House. It was built to provide protection against possible attacks during the Indian trouble in 1860. *(Courtesy of Nevada Historical Society)*

The Trimmer House

T HE RANCH NOW owned by Genoa historian Arnold Trimmer on the eastern edge of the town is the original Claim Number One, the pre-emption claim of Colonel John Reese recorded in the First Records of Carson Valley on December 1, 1852. It was purchased by Arnold's father, Robert Trimmer, on August 16, 1909, from Lawrence Frey. Mr. Frey, a colorful character of pioneer days, errant but nevertheless lovable, was a teamster in Genoa in 1861. The house was built by Mr. Frey in 1885.

In 1877 Mr. Frey opened the New Pioneer Butcher Shop built of brick near the corner of Nixon and Main Streets. This step was taken following an unsuccessful venture in Placerville from which he was rescued by his faithful wife and her dear friend, the seeress Eilley Orrum Bowers, once the mistress of Bower's Mansion in Washoe Valley. As the story goes, Mr. Frey, always industrious and enterprising, experienced a lull in business in Genoa. He hoped to do better in Placerville, whither he went, leaving his family at home. After receiving a few glowing letters but no money to run her home and take care of the children, Mrs. Frey became desperate. She confided her anxiety to her friend, Mrs. Bowers, who gazed into her crystal ball where she saw dimly at first what appeared to be a long table. As the vision became clearer, it resembled a twenty-

four foot bar and the absent husband was at the end with a glass in his hand surrounded by convivial company. Mrs. Frey took appropriate action forthwith.

Some years later, in 1890, while Mr. Frey was delivering meat to a mining camp, his older daughter eloped with a young musician who, accompanied by his brother, had come to town with a traveling circus. The two "clowns," as Mr. Frey dubbed them, George and Charley Brown, roomed and boarded with Mr. and Mrs. Frey. On his return home and the discovery of the romantic exploit of his daughter, the enraged Mr. Frey ran upstairs to the room of the despised tootlers, seized his son-in-law's horn, carried it to the front porch and to the refrain of "Damn the Musicians," stamped it flat. However, he received his daughter and her husband kindly when they returned from their honeymoon.

A runaway marriage in his family was not the only event that could enrage Mr. Frey. Indeed, Wesley Walker, a lifelong resident of Genoa, recalls how natural phenomena could also raise Mr. Frey's ire. When Wesley was a small boy, a cloudburst occurred causing a flood. Mr. Frey was trying with all his energy and ingenuity to turn the raging waters of Genoa Creek away from his small diversion ditch and keep them in the main channel. Each shovel full of dirt washed out faster than the last. At length, to his astonishment, the small Wesley saw the enraged man tear off his hat, stomp on it and finally in desperation lie down in the stream. When the juvenile observer rushed forward to question his actions, Mr. Frey drove him away with a threat to cut his throat. Needless to say, the boy ran;

hence history does not tell us how this battle with the elements terminated.

Mr. Frey could be moved to tears as well as anger. As a lad in Genoa, he was a contemporary of that colorful gambler and friend of the underdog, "Lucky Bill" Thorington, who was also a prominent settler on the Carson River Route. When "Lucky Bill" was sentenced to be hanged by the vigilantes, (calling themselves the "Committee") for harboring a murderer, young Frey and several other youths to whom the alleged miscreant was a hero, joined the crowd of anxious citizens that followed the "Committee" on the way to the site of the hanging. The "Committee," all young men in their twenties and thirties, who hanged their prisoner on that regrettable day in July 1858, forced the protesting Lawrence to mount the wagon on which "Lucky Bill" stood in the shadow of the gallows and to take in his hands the reins of the team of mules. When the weeping teenager hesitated, "Lucky Bill" came to the rescue with his unfailing gallantry: "Drive out, Boy," he said.

Miss Mary Davies (*Courtesy of Ione Hawkins Fettic*)

The Kinsey House

IF THE WALLS of this charming old house could speak, they would tell tales of adventure spanning three continents. Sarah Jane Thompson, its first mistress, was brought from Ireland to the United States when an infant in arms by her mother, Mary McGee Thompson. Mary, at this time, was the widow of Captain Thompson of the British Army who lost his life while serving on the frontiers of India in the first Afghan War (1838-1842).

In these sad circumstances, Mary packed her trunks and with tiny Sarah Jane in her arms joined a party of emigrants going to the United States.

Proceeding by boat inland from New York, Mary and Sarah Jane were in a shipwreck on Lake Erie. Mary was ill at the time. A woman passenger, taking advantage of this double calamity and capitalizing on her friendship stole Mary's trunks. Then with the other passengers, this "friend" abandoned the young mother and her infant daughter to the waves. A Negro looter came out to salvage what he could from the wreck. Touched by the plight of Mary and her tiny daughter, he took them to shore and to the home of John Hawkins in Perry, Lake County, Ohio. Mr. Hawkins' wife had recently died in childbirth and he needed someone to care for his infant son. After a few months John Hawkins and Mary Thompson were married.

About twelve years later, the Hawkins family crossed the plains to Carson Valley. There Sarah Jane grew up to become the bride of Stephen A. Kinsey in 1856, and to live in the house he built for her of brick from the kiln on Boyd Lane. In this stately abode and with innate dignity, Sarah Jane in the years following ascended and descended the beautiful stairway with its skillfully mitered corners built by her stepfather, John Hawkins.

In 1860, during the Indian troubles of that year, Sarah Jane suffered another miraculous escape. In May guards were thrown around the town of Genoa and provision made to have the women, in case of attack, seek shelter in the stone basement of merchants Mandelbaum and Klauber.

Late one afternoon, a wanderer made his way into the settlement, seeking shelter from the Indians. He was given permission to sleep in a partially completed building. That night he had a dream that Indians were killing him and jumping up in his sleep he started for the door. He struck his head against a timber and was knocked down. Regaining his feet and with blood running freely from the wound in his forehead, he fled towards the mountain, yelling, "Injun, Injun." He was stopped by one of the guards; frantically he told how he had been attacked by a murderous Indian.

The alarm was given; the women were aroused from their slumbers and hurried to the stone basement. During the excitement, a lady whose husband was prominent in affairs of the early-day settlement, upon reaching the shelter, remembered that she (we think it was Sarah Jane) had left a pair of new hoops at her home; she begged her husband to risk his life to recover the hoops. While she

The Douglas Seminary, a private school situated in the Kinsey Gardens. *(Courtesy of Lena Gardelli Falcke)*

Stephen A. Kinsey home in Genoa before remodeling.

The Kinsey House, home of Stephen A. Kinsey. Kinsey was recorder of Carson County, Utah Territory, and later auditor of Douglas County, State of Nevada. The house came into possession of Mr. and Mrs. Emory Marshall on September 20, 1949. They remodeled the interior and built onto the rear of the old house, preserving the original appearance of the front. The house was bought by Minor and Maxine Kelso, in 1970. They are converting it and the extensive grounds, known in pioneer days as the Kinsey Gardens, to a club with guest accommodations known as Sierra Shadows. *(Courtesy of James A. Lawrence)*

was still pleading, word was sent about town that the alarm was false. The lady's life, and her hoops also, were spared!

After this near-tragedy, Mr. and Mrs. Kinsey led a gracious life in their lovely home, typified in summer by the account of a garden party held in August of 1880 attended by Judge Beatty and Attorney-General Slater. Dancing continued into the early hours of Sunday morning when a silver cake dish was awarded the most graceful couple. However, there lurked beneath this social image a certain lack of domestic harmony which may have been compensated for in the life of Mr. Kinsey by the arrival in 1879 of his cousin Mary Davies, an accomplished lady from New York who, in 1882, became head-mistress of the Genoa or Douglas Seminary situated in the Kinsey Gardens.

Stephen Kinsey preserved his equanamity and zest for living into the nineties of the last century being frequently seen of a winter's day on the streets of Genoa, "cutting quite a dash" in his stylish sleigh drawn by his high-stepping buggy horse.

The Genoa Fire

MANY ARE the tales told of that disastrous day, June 28, 1910, when the greater part of the business district of Genoa burned. The Poor House (the historic Nevada Hotel in 1862 and later Gilman's Hotel) was where the fire started from a pan of sulphur one of the inmates was burning under his bed to kill the bedbugs. The fire was whipped northward along the street by a heavy gale. Burned were Hansen's Saloon, the Odd Fellows Hall, the Union Church and, finally, the combustible portions of the County Court House. Flying shingles carried the flames across the street to ancient landmarks in Block 13, such as Gelatt's Barn which was then owned by Sheriff Wyatt, Hansen's Hall, Gray's Blacksmith Shop and the Genoa Fort which had been built by Colonel Reese in 1851. The county records were rushed into the new fireproof vault recently constructed of reinforced concrete; the Gardnerville

The court house after the fire of 1910.

The Gelatt livery stable or barn burning. *(Courtesy of Arnold Trimmer)*

Those present at a day in court posed before the rebuilt court house: Left to right: Hans R. Jepsen, Attorney George A. Montrose, Judge Frank P. Langan, Felice Cohen (court reporter), Hans C. Jepsen (county clerk), Andy Arrild (sheriff), Al Jarvis, Joe Cardinal, Wm. Dangberg, Ezra Jarvis, Judge Daniel Webster Virgin, Frank Jones, Frank Brockliss (district attorney), T.P. Hawkins. *(Courtesy of Hans R. Jepsen)*

The Gelatt livery and feed stable, known as the Tingham livery stable in 1862, was purchased by the Gelatt brothers in 1874. It stood on the east side of Main Street across from the court house. It was burned in the fire of 1910. *(Courtesy of the Nevada State Historical Society)*

The blacksmith shop of William Daniel Gray was originally owned by James W. McLean, member of the legislative assembly of Nevada Territory in 1861. In the door are W.D. Gray with son William Joseph in the white hat and son Morton Thomas in the dark hat. In the buggy is Frank Walker, whose father was the wheelwright in the Gray shop. It stood on the east side of Main Street north of the stockade. It was burned in the fire of 1910. *(Courtesy of Dr. M.A. Johnsen)*

Among those standing in this 1885 photo are: Wm. Selby, R. Gelatt, Albert Daudel, Frank Walker, Ed Whitemere, Wally Gelatt, Will Gray, Felix Martin, Gear Lowe, Edgar Seaman, Henry Rice, George Van Sickle, Harry Van Sickle, Maurice Falk, Tom Laurie, Lyle Burnham, Sam Harris, Leon Hawkins, Harry Osborn and Ed Scranton. (*Courtesy of Alan Van Sickle*)

Fire Department started racing across the valley with its hand-pumped fire engine drawn by two relays of galloping horses; Sheriff Wyatt started for home from Carson where he had gone on business with his team of horses galloping all the way; garden hoses were brought into play on roofs and, in some miraculous way, the rest of the town was saved.

Untold in history books is the tale of the rite performed a block away from the fire by the famous hostess of the Raycraft Exchange, Mrs. Ellen Raycraft, then in her ninetieth year. All unobserved by the frantic fire-fighters, both men and women, this pioneer lady with admirable faith did her part. She was raised a Catholic; her eleven children had been baptised in the Church but not confirmed.

Nevertheless, she had always kept on hand a large bottle of Holy Water on the shelf beside the alcohol. One or the other had aided over the years in the happy resolution of many a domestic crisis. This was indeed a crisis that no one could dispute. Ellen, clad in her dark shirt waist dress with apron, kerchief and shawl all in place as usual, took the bottle of Holy Water from its shelf and, holding it in her left hand, went out into the smoke and ash-filled air. Cupping her right hand she filled it and scattered the contents to the wind. This act she repeated again and again as she walked around the borders of the Raycraft property. As the afternoon shadows fell over the devastated old town the usual evening breeze wafted down the Genoa Canyon and all to the south was saved!

Raycraft's Exchange, built in the early 1860s. It and the livery stable, just to the north across Mill Street were purchased from D.W. Virgin on February 15, 1868. Joseph Raycraft and his wife Ellen operated the hostelry from 1866 until 1910 after which date it was torn down. *(Courtesy of Josephine Raycraft Hellwinkel)*

GENOA, _July 17_ 188_

Mr. J. Darling

Bought of **MANDLEBAUM & KLAUBER,**

WHOLESALE AND RETAIL DEALERS IN

GROCERIES, PROVISIONS, WINES, LIQUORS,

CIGARS, CLOTHING, DRY GOODS, BOOTS, SHOES, HARDWARE, DRUGS,

Medicines, Paints, Oils, Glass, Crockery, Stoves, Tinware, Furniture, Saddlery, Farmers' and Mining Implements, Toys, Etc.,

MAIN STREET, GENOA, C. V.

Orders from a distance promptly attended to.

2.5	Green Coffee	4	6 2 7	
1	for pounds		1 —	
3	Bottle Mustard	2		
1	Scythe & Snathe		3	
2	Rakes	7	3	
1	Forth			
			14 7 5	
	Price			
	Mandleham		Klauber	
			B Klauber	

GLIMPSES ALONG THE CARSON RIVER ROUTE

Walley Hot Springs

IN THE SERVICE of truth and not, as it might appear, to cast doubt on the veracity of the lady who was offering this property for sale in settlement of her husband's estate, we subscribe quotes to this challenging statement. The advertisement for sale on the Tenth Day of July, 1876, continues: "After being given up as incurables by the 'most eminent physicians on the Pacific Coast and elsewhere' thousands of persons have found that the 'magic waters' seldom failed to cure 'rheumatism, syphilis, dropsy, gout, Bright's disease of the kidneys, dyspepsia and hundreds of the diseases which flesh is heir to, and particularly all scrofulous affections'."

Witness to the efficacy of the Springs in treating a more universal ailment is bourne by a traveler to Washoe in the reverse gold rush from California to the Comstock in 1860. John Ross Browne, author and humorist, who had been ailing, undertook the journey from Sacramento to Washoe in search of health and, hopefully, fortune. On foot he entered Hope Valley and Woodfords Canyon in a terrific windstorm and blinding sleet. Staggering forward for six miles, he and his companions reached the first station in Carson Valley at the foot of the Canyon. Browne says: "I had endured the journey thus far very well, and had gained considerably in strength and appetite. The next day, however, upon striking into the sand of Carson Valley, my feet became terribly blistered, and the walking was exceedingly painful. By sundown I had made only 15 miles and still was three miles from Genoa. Every hundred yards was now equal to a mile. At length I found it utterly impossible to move another step. It was quite dark and there

Walley Hot Springs about 1875. *(Courtesy of Ed and Helen Johnson)*

was nothing for it but to sit down on the roadside. Fortunately, the weather was comparatively mild. As I was meditating how to pass the night, I perceived a hot spring close by, toward which I crept; and finding the water strongly impregnated with salt, it occurred to me that it might benefit my feet. I soon plunged them in, and in half an hour found them so much improved that I was enabled to resume my journey. An hour more and I was snugly housed in Genoa.''

Two years later, David Walley who, in 1860, had responded to the call of Washoe from his home in New York, also noted the excellence of the springs. He sent for his wife, Harriet, and together during the next thirteen years they caused a ''magnificent'' hotel, stabling and ball room to arise from a mere rock pile on the emigrant road. With never-failing industry and enthusiasm they converted the surrounding burnt-up tule beds into beautiful flower

Reproduction of picture post card of Walley Hot Springs about 1905. *(Courtesy of Nevada State Park Commission)*

and useful vegetable gardens. The Walleys not only provided delightful physical surroundings for their clientele but, as reported by a traveler in 1869, they also kept a physician in residence to serve their guests. To ensure the benefits of the mud baths to patrons, masseurs were also employed. One of these, in the 1880's, was a young man from Denmark, Hans Christian Jessen, who later became an innkeeper and a miner.

David Walley's untimely death on March 6, 1875 left his widow in possession of the hostelry, ''elegant'' for those days, the furnishings of which are described in the administratix' notice: The parlor was graced with two fine sofas, three large easy chairs, six hair-bottom chairs, one double rocking chair, a stove, five sets of window curtains, a what-not, one marble-top center table, and one marble-top stand, two spittoons, two rugs, carpet on the floor and a stationary lamp. The forty bedrooms were furnished with the following essentials: double or single beds with springs, straw and moss mattresses, two pairs white blankets, spread and feather pillows, washstand, bowl and pitcher, complete in each. And there were eleven bathrooms, containing glass and comb in each!

It was asserted at the time of Mr. Walley's death that

View of Walley Hot Springs about 1905.

there had been a hundred thousand dollars spent on the resort. On December 5, 1879, the personal property of David Walley was sold under court order for support of his family. Finally, after her death on December 9, 1896, the resort was sold by Harriet Walley's heirs, in November 1897, to John and Richard Raycraft for $5000. Somewhat later, Jane Raycraft and her husband James R. Campbell purchased the resort and operated it until 1906.

One of the resort's most permanent features, the large stone cold cellar, survived the fire that destroyed the resort in part and also escaped the demolition in 1929-1930. It has been turned into a bar adjoining the dining room operated since 1958 by Ed and Helen Johnson.

Van Sickle Station

VAN SICKLE Station, the largest hostelry on the Carson River Route, stood just to the south of Walley's and to the north of the Daggett Pass Trail. Henry Van Sickle was born in New Jersey and came to Genoa in 1852 where he traded with Indians and immigrants. In 1855, he took up a claim where his station stood and had Charles Holbrook build him a house on it in 1857, the nucleus of the well-known station. This was a far-seeing move on the part of Van Sickle and also indicates how well informed he was concerning the interest in California at that time in opening up a wagon road to Carson Valley. Mr. Van Sickle was well established on his new claim three years before the opening up of the road over the Daggett Pass by Kingsbury and McDonald.

About 1860 there were five barns at the station. Each night these were filled with horses and mules. Other freight teams, the overflow, were tied to the surrounding corrals.

After a night of munching hay which was hauled in bales to the barns by many of the neighboring ranchers, the teams, amid vast volleys of oaths, were harnessed and led around to tongues of the freight wagons to be hitched up for the next leg of the journey whether westward over the pass toward Placerville or northward along the Carson River to Carson and Virginia cities. Moving among the teamsters, the loaded wagons and the horses and mules was the respected and picturesque proprietor Henry Van Sickle with one pant leg stuffed into his boot top, the other hanging loose. To inquiries concerning this curious sartorial habit he is said to have replied that by this device he would be easily distinguished from others and easily identified. Another distinguishing mark was the bucket he carried which served as a portable cash register and into which was dumped the tariff for the night's accommodation of both man and beast. It is known that his revenue from the operation of the station was about one thousand dollars a day. Another source of revenue was the sale of hay, meat and other produce to the merchants of Virginia City. One very large collection from this source he buried; when he went to recover it, however, he could not find it. All this was changed when the mines on the Comstock fell into evil days beginning in 1879.

Henry Van Sickle was a man of many skills that were of signal importance in service to persons living on the Carson River Route. He came west as a teamster, began life in Carson Valley as a small trader, was a blacksmith by trade and operated a blacksmith shop at his station in which he employed several men. He was an innkeeper and, at one time, became a justice of the peace. Several times he served on the board of county commissioners for Douglas County and he also served as county treasurer. He was a practical engineer for many years and kept the channel of the East Fork of the Carson River properly aligned. Like many other men with financial know-how, Mr. Van Sickle was also a sort of amateur banker, making loans

Henry Van Sickle. *(Courtesy of Alan Van Sickle)*

Approaching Van Sickle Station from the north. In the foreground is one of the five barns of the original station. *(Courtesy of James A. Lawrence)*

The Van Sickle Station Hotel built by Charles Holbrook in 1857. Just north of the hotel are the stone warehouse and blacksmith shop. Buildings on the left behind the hotel were for help, principally Chinese. The hotel was torn down many years ago. *(Courtesy of Alan Van Sickle)*

The Henry Van Sickle family and Dr. Luce at their home in Genoa. Earlier this was the house where A.C. Pratt published the Carson Valley News 1875-1879. *(Courtesy of Alan Van Sickle)*

The Van Sickle Station blacksmith shop before restoration by Mr. and Mrs. Fritz Ruppel after 1944. *(Courtesy of Juanita Schubert)*

on property. He was also an early day real estate broker, buying and selling ranch and town property.

A story often told by William Trimmer gives a glimpse into the character of this prominent pioneer who could rise to the occasion when a word spoken in jest turned the joke on himself. Young William, who was for a number of years employed by Mr. Van Sickle as a teamster, was driving a wagon and back-action loaded with baled hay to the station one day. His destination was the barn on the hillside far above the emigrant road — the barn Mr. Van Sickle reserved for his own horses. To reach this barn, William had to negotiate a U-turn and pass through a gate. His employer, watching the delicate maneuver from above the turn, called out, "Go ahead, take the gate post out." This, despite his best efforts, young William proceeded to do. In fear and trembling he drove on toward the barn, hearing to his surprise the injured party call out, "That's right, you did what I told you to do! Now go on, unhitch your horses, put them in the barn to feed and, when you are all through, come down to the bar where there will be a drink waiting for you."

The stone store, warehouse, bar and blacksmith buildings of the Van Sickle Station were restored, after purchase in 1944, as a private residence by Mr. and Mrs. Fritz Ruppel. The large two-story frame house, built in 1857, which served as the hotel, was torn down after 1909.

The Georgetown Trail — The Kingsbury Grade

PASSING SMOOTHLY over the Kingsbury Grade from Tahoe to Carson Valley, the motorist is using in part the Georgetown Trail of early immigrant days, so named for the reason that near Rubicon Point on the southwest shore of Lake Tahoe, it joined the trail to the Mother Lode town of Georgetown, which was situated approximately 15 miles east of Auburn, California. The name of Daggett was attached to this trail when Dr. C. D. Daggett, in 1854, staked out a claim to 640 acres embracing its debouchment. After this considerable acquisition the name Georgetown gave way to that of Daggett Trail and Pass.

In 1855, the Daggett Trail was described by George Goddard in words that would be recognized by today's motorist:

"Descending to the valley, the barometer made the height of this pass above Daggett's, 2,407 feet, the distance is under four miles; the trail is in some places very precipitious, and winds along the steep sides of the mountain, where a false step would precipitate one into the rocky canyon 500 feet below."

When it was opened in 1860, the local correspondent of the *San Francisco Herald* (issue of September 15, 1860) reported:

"I have heretofore mentioned the new wagon road of Kingsbury and McDonald, extending seven miles in length, from Carson Valley to Lake Valley. I have since had an

Job's Peak seen from the Kingsbury Grade. (*Courtesy of James A. Lawrence*)

44

opportunity of examining the work and could not but admire the skill with which these gentlemen have wound around seemingly impassable heights with a most excellent road. The distance to Placerville is now reduced some fifteen miles, and so far as the difference in time is concerned, everybody admits that to heavy teams a day's travel is saved. The rates of toll are reasonable.''

Snow plant in bloom. *(Courtesy of Juanita Schubert)*

Two years before completion of the Kingsbury Toll Road, improvements at a cost of $24,800 had been made on the western end of the Carson Valley Wagon Road, all except the Brockliss Bridge over the south fork of the American River. In 1859, however, it was reported that the road to Carson Valley was in a deplorable condition and it was suggested that it become a toll road paid for by teamsters and not immigrants. Hence it may be assumed that completion, in 1860, of the eastern end of the Carson Valley Wagon Road was a welcome event.

Almost immediately after its opening the Kingsbury Toll Road became the route of the Pony Express, replacing the Carson (Woodfords) Canyon route used for a few months from April 1860 until the new road was available. In addition to the Concord coaches which carried passengers between Genoa and Placerville and the freight wagons carrying goods, an important use of the road was for the driving of livestock — cattle, sheep, hogs — to the markets in Virginia City. J.W. Haines, later a resident of Genoa, tells how in the late months of 1859 he waited in Lake Valley with a band of 500 sheep for the opening of the new road. He said another drover also waited with 100 fat hogs. The Kingsbury, however, opened too late for these men.

The Snow Plant

WHAT A STARTLING, thrilling sight it must have been for the pioneer travelers plodding wearily up the Daggett's Pass Trail to come upon these flashing red plants at the edge of the melting snowbanks. They were called *gewe mukus* by the Washoe Indians.

Of this plant, Helen Hunt Jackson was prompted to write: ''Surely there can be no flower on earth whose look so allies it to uncanny beings and powers. 'Sarcodes sanguinea' the botanists have called it. Imagine a red cone, from four to ten inches in height, and one or two in diameter, set firmly in the ground. It is not only simply red, it is blood-red; deep and bright as drops from living veins. It is soft, fleshlike, and in the beginning shows simply a surface of small, close, lapping, sheath-like points, as a pinecone does. These slowly open, beginning at the top, and as they fold back you see under each one a small flower, shaped like the flower of the Indian pipe, and of similar pulpiness. This also is blood-red; but the center of the cone, now revealed, is of a fleshy-pinkish white; so also is the tiny, almost imperceptible stem which unites the flower to it. They grow sometimes in clumps, sometimes singly. As far off as one can see into the dim vistas of these pine forests there will gleam out the vivid scarlet of one of these superb, uncanny flowers. When its time comes to die, it turns black, so that in its death, also, it looks like a fleshy thing linked to mysteries.'' (From George Wharton James, *California Romantic and Beautiful*, pp. 346-347.)

45

The Fleabane

THIS CHARMING blue-lavender aster-like flower, perched precariously in the crevice of a granite boulder on the eastern slope of the Sierra, extends an irresistible invitation to the photographer who would preserve a record of its daring, one might almost say its imagination, its sense of the dramatic, in having sought a home in a spoonful of soil high above the floor of Carson Valley. Many of its kind grow below in the decomposed granite along the mountainside where silken-tasseled seeds wafted in the breeze, but less daring than this one, come to rest to produce plants that afforded the pioneers their insect repellant. Bunches hung in cabins or burned in them drove out the pestiferous bugs, particularly the fleas; hence the name *Fleabane*, bane of fleas.

The Fleabane clinging to a granite wall. *(Courtesy of Juanita Schubert)*

Sunflowers. *(Courtesy of Juanita Schubert)*

Sunflowers

ABOUT MID-SUMMER this bright yellow flower appears along roadsides in cultivated and uncultivated fields in Carson Valley. It is a sun-worshipper and in the bud stage faces east following the course of its god from east to west where it rests at the end of the day. At midnight the bud slowly begins to gyrate eastward where it reverently awaits the return of the sun. This continues daily until the bud begins to open. And so the romantic ballad of an earlier age celebrates a fact of nature

The sunflower turns on her god when he sets

The same look which she turned when he rose.

The Washoes called the plant "madukwahlu." They gathered the ripened seeds, dried them, then pounded them with a muller to break the shells which they ground into flour to make a palatable porridge.

Rabbit Brush

WITH THE ARRIVAL of September, Carson Valley is ornamented with a crown of gold, the blooming brush — *chrysothamnus* to the botanist, *bopo* or rubber brush to the Washoe Indians. Every gravelly flat and every foothill around the green fields are covered with this final blaze of color as though Nature had hoarded its energy through spring and summer to provide a golden spectacle just before the onset of winter. Its clustered flower heads provide honey to the bees and a yellow dye to the Indians. Its stalks with their knots and bumps provide chewing gum to the Indian children and speculation to the scientists who find considerable high grade rubber in the plant.

Rabbit Brush. *(Courtesy of Edith Amanda Mereen)*

Cattails

THE CATTAILS of Carson Valley's swamps provided a stone age supermarket to the original inhabitants, the Washoe Indians, who called them *mahat alal* and attributed to them a primary role in the creation of man. Thus did primitive man combine the utilitarian properties of what the botanist calls *typha latifolia* with a mysterious power — the power of transmutation, with the assistance of magical ritual, of seeds into men.

The uses of the plant are impressive: in early spring the young tender leaf shoots are eaten raw or cooked; the flowering stalks, gathered before the pollen has developed, are a great delicacy also eaten raw or cooked. These were relished by the pioneers who called them "Cossack asparagus." When the flower spikes are mature they are filled with pollen. The Washoes harvested vast quantitites of this fine golden flour with which to make bread or mush or tasty bars for the children to nibble. The Indian children even today enjoy the sticky sweet sap of the stems. The dried stalks were used not only as food, but also as building material to cover the willow frames of wiki-ups. And finally the drug-counter of this stone age supermarket pro-

Cattails. *(Courtesy of Juanita Schubert)*

Flouring Mills

GRIST OR flouring mills, together with sawmills, were among the first manufacturing establishments to be built in Carson Valley. These mills served the emigrants moving along the Carson River Route as well as the settlers who ran the stations to accommodate them. The first mill was built by millwright Thomas J. Knott for Colonel John Reese. It stood on Mill Street in Genoa and began converting wheat to flour in 1854. The first wheat to be ground was brought south from Honey Lake, California. Soon, however, the settlers began to grow their own small plots of grain.

The second mill in Carson Valley was built by millwright Sam Silliman for Hiram Mott of Mottsville. Situated on Mott Creek just north of the hamlet of Mottsville, it was built around 1857 or 1858.

In 1865 the Reese mill was purchased by William M. Cary who came to Carson Valley from Placerville where he had owned the so-called Cary House. He moved the mill from Genoa to the foot of the Kingsbury Grade where it stood for many years. In 1874 it came into the possession of Robert Falcke and was henceforth known as the Farmers' Mill. It was still in operation in the early 1900s.

It was some years later in 1895 when the Douglas Flour Mill was built on Long Valley Creek just above where it flows into the East Fork of the Carson River. This was a very ambitious undertaking as the account of it in the *Genoa Courier* indicates. On May 24, 1895, it was reported that one-half of the machinery for the new mill, weighing thirty thousand pounds, had arrived in Carson City on the Virginia and Truckee Railroad and was being unloaded at Peterson's Hay Yard on four wagons for delivery to the mill in Carson Valley. The same notice asserted that the mill was a three-story structure, machinery was of the roller pattern, the capacity of the mill was fifty barrels per day and the cost was $20,000. This mill made flour under the brand name *Ladies' Best*; Fred W. Sarman was the miller.

The machinery of the Douglas Flour Mill was moved to Gardnerville in 1912. The new mill building was financed by J.N. Anderson; Fred W. Sarman supplied the equipment; the mill still made flour under the label *Ladies' Best*.

Two other mills were built in Carson Valley. In January of 1900 the Eagle Roller Mill Company was founded by W.F. Dressler, Henry and H.H. Beck. This mill was built north of Genoa on Adams Creek. Six years later William F. Dressler, H.F. Dangberg, Jr., Richard Bassman, H.H. Springmeyer and C.M. Henningsen incorporated the Minden Flour Milling Company which became the Minden Milling Company in 1942, when it was converted to a livestock feed mill which still operates under this name.

In contrast to the grinding and refining machinery shipped into Carson Valley for these later mills is Thomas Knott's description of the grinding stones installed in the

vided its patrons with cattail leaves, burned to charcoal and finely powdered to be applied, according to directions, to bleeding navels and other bleeding parts. It also recommended that the stalks before flowering could be used as a cure for diarrhea.

Modern man has added uses for the cattail, suggested by research at Syracuse University where the rhizome was ground into flour suitable for making cookies or a substitute for cornstarch. It may also be fermented to produce ethyl alcohol or used for growing molds from which antibiotics are made.

Practical uses, long practiced, are the caulking of barrels with the stems and the caulking of the staves with the leaves. Pioneer women in the fall harvested the strong stems of the flower stalks for candle molds. The leaves are suitable for making rush-bottom chairs and baskets as well as insulating material. And last but not least, small boys in the last century soaked the cattail heads in kerosene, lighted them and waved the flaming torches in political parades.

The Cary Mill, later the Falcke Mill at the foot of Kingsbury Grade. The miller's dwelling behind the mill was the toll house for the road. *(Courtesy of Lean Gardelli Falcke)*

The Douglas Flour Mill in 1895. *(Courtesy of Henry and Edna Frevert)*

Flour mill of the Douglas Milling and Power Company in Gardnerville. In front, a ten-horse team and wagons loading sacks of flour or grain. *(Courtesy of Henry and Edna Frevert)*

The Minden Flour Milling Company's mill and grain storage tanks about 1925.

first flouring or grist mill, the Reese mill, built by him in Genoa in 1854 and removed to the foot of Kingsbury in 1865. According to Knott, it was operated with two buhr stones, referred to as a run of buhrs. The bottom one was stationary while the top one turned. They were about five feet in diameter and ten to twelve inches thick. The stone was a cream-colored knotty porous quartz which had to be imported from Scotland, France or England. The stones came in fifty or sixty pound sections to be fitted together at the scene of construction, like keystones, to make the larger circle. These sections of stone, carried over the Sierra Nevada on muleback, gave the pioneers of Carson Valley, in 1854 and for many years after, their vitamin-rich stone ground flour!

Sawmills

THE SAWMILL shown in action in the picture below was producing lumber in 1900. It stood at the foot of a canyon north of Mottsville and is typical of other mills which were operated along the Carson River Route on the lower slopes of the Sierra Nevada. The first of these was built in 1853 by millwright Thomas Knott at the mouth of the Carson (Woodfords) Canyon. In his diary Knott says that in March of 1853 he and two other men, carrying their blankets and provisions strapped on their backs, started back across the Sierra Nevada from California. Knott had entered California in 1852 by way

of Carson Valley where he had observed the numerous clear streams flowing from the mountains.

Coming back into the valley, Knott found, lying where they had been abandoned by the emigrants, all the tools he needed to ply his trade. The story is continued in Knott's own words:

"So I set my stakes and went to work, as there was a fine flat of pine timber on the South Side of the Creek. At the latter end of May the mountains got so a pack train could cross, so I had my Mill irons packed over; a mill crank that weighed 190 lbs., and all the other mill irons that we needed; a blacksmith anvil, vice and tools. As for wrought iron we had all we needed from Emigrant wagons that had been burnt. I gathered up 400 wagon tires and other wagon irons, and gathered together 40 or 50 log chains. In July, I started the saw to sawing lumber before Migration came in from the states and Salt Lake. There were no mills at that time in what is now the state of Nevada.

"This mill was run by a flutter wheel and an upright sash saw, twenty-four foot head and fall."

Knott and associate John L. Cary (or Carey) sold this mill in 1853 to "Lucky Bill" Thorington. It continued to be called the Cary Mill. Near it was the hostelry known as the Cary House.

In 1854 Knott built a sawmill for Colonel John Reese at the mouth of Mill Creek Canyon (later known as Genoa Creek) in Genoa. By 1862 this mill was being used as a jail, eloquent testimony to the speed with which a mill could wipe out the surrounding forest.

Another sawmill was built in 1858 by Ira M. Luther in Luther Canyon (sometimes called Fay Canyon) which

The Hanson and Park Sawmill in operation about 1904 in a canyon just north of Mottsville. (Courtesy of Beatrice Fettic Jones)

Elzy Knott, his wife Mary (Harris) and his daughter Elzyette at age twelve. She was adopted by William Williams whom her mother married after the death of Elzy. In 1860, during the Indian troubles, Mary fled on horseback to Strawberry on the Genoa Placerville Road, carrying her infant daughter in her arms. *(Courtesy of Juanita Jarvis Malo)*

was operated by an overshot water wheel, utilizing the waters of the canyon. Remains of this old mill may still be seen.

Other sawmills of early days were those situated in the vicinity of Fredericksburg, one on the north in Gibbs Canyon and one on the south in Dry Canyon. A one-quarter interest in the Gibbs Canyon mill was sold by millwright Sam Silliman to Patrick Canady in 1864; the remaining three-quarters interest was sold, in the same year, by three citizens of Fredericksburg among whom was a Frederick Biggershof (or Brickerhof) — the eponymous settler of Fredericksburg — and eventually also came into the hands of Patrick Canady. The story is adapted from the account of Sara Elizabeth (Neddenriep) Lampe, preserving her sprightly comment.

Patrick Canady seems to have hung on until May 27, 1868, when he sold 484 acres of land and the Cast Iron Sawmill to Jackson S. Wright. Here the sawmill begins to withdraw from the spotlight, reappearing the following year, 1869, as the Fredericksburg Mill Company. Taxes were paid on the following: "The right of possession in and to one timber tract, situated at the mouth of Gibbs Canyon, west of the town of Fredericksburg, with sawmill and other improvements thereon. Lumber, one wagon, eight oxen, one horse, furniture."

In 1870, the mill was in still more modest circumstances. The owner paid taxes "on the right of possession in and

to one tract of land containing fifty acres, situated west of the town of Fredericksburg, and bounded on the north by the Widow Gibbs ranch (part of Chris Gansberg's place), on the south by Woodfords ranch (part of the Hubert Bruns place), together with house and other improvements, wagon $25, furniture $25, tools $10, personal property $10, hay and grain.'' "Who ate those oxen?'' asks Mrs. Lampe.

Built in 1854, the Reese Mill was the bone of contention in one of the bitterest of early-day lawsuits, that of millwright Knott versus mill owner Reese for the cost of building the mill. The effect of this suit on the town of Genoa is told by "Tennessee," local correspondent of the *San Francisco Herald* (issue of April 3, 1860). He says that a heavy suit was pending against the Mormons — that is, Colonel Reese and his associates, and that the whole town was under attachment. He concludes, "consequently, no title can now be had to lots here for building." Aside from the frustrating effect this litigation had on property and would-be property owners in the town of Genoa, it fanned flames of anger and gave rise to such bitterness between the principals that it carried over to their descendants who saw all the world in terms of Mormon versus "Gentile." The coloration of these factions was either black or white depending on the side to which one thought his ancestors belonged.

When millwright Knott was unable to get all of his expected money from Reese for building the mill, he returned to Ohio, leaving his son Elzy in Genoa to do

Elzyette in her later years when she, as Mrs. Selby, was sought out by visitors to Genoa to answer questions concerning pioneer days. She died in 1944. *(Courtesy of Nevada State Highway Department)*

the collecting. He came again to Carson Valley on the 1st of February 1859. At this time Elzy Knott, the handsomest man in Genoa, a six-footer with curly brown hair, had obtained judgment for $20,000 against Reese. He had also acquired a wife who came to Carson Valley from South Wales in 1856.

Mary Harris was a waitress in one of the hotels at Woodfords when Elzy Knott came courting. The young couple spent much of their time together on long horseback rides. One day, in August 1857, they were riding along the emigrant road past the Van Sickle Station when Elzy said to Mary, "Let's get married. There's Henry over there in the field branding cattle." She accepted him; they got down from their horses and called Henry who had been elected Justice of the Peace in 1855. The men helping Henry all stopped branding, so the story goes, to come over and see the wedding. "And," concluded the narrator, Elzy's daughter, "that's how they got married."

On March 8, 1859, a young Mormon named John Herring shot and killed Elzy when the latter entered his house to retrieve a bridle involved in a gambling dispute. Elzy's grave is in Genoa in a sagebrush field. Elzy's daughter Elzyette was born seven months later on October 12, 1859. She later became the well-known pioneer lady, Mrs. William Selby of Genoa.

An even more notorious dispute over non-payment for sawmills inspired in 1862 the so-called "curse" pronounced by Probate Judge and Mormon elder, Orson Hyde. Though the mill was situated in Washoe Valley, Hyde included Carson Valley in his malediction, a version of which follows:

The Curse of Orson Hyde

A version prepared from the original by Patricia Frevert Allen

1. And it came to pass that Orson Hyde was sent by the Mormons out from Utah into Carson Valley.

2. For in the year 1854, Hyde had been named probate judge of Carson County.

2a. And he came to Carson County in 1855 and remained two years.

3. And during that time, Hyde determined to build a saw mill.

4. He reared up large beams and built a saw mill which was exceedingly great.

5. And two years having past, Hyde was returned by the church from his duties in Carson Valley, back into Utah.

6. Now, at the end of seven years, Hyde sent a message in writing unto the people of Carson Valley for he was greatly wroth.

7. And he said unto them, Woe to the people who dwell in Carson Valley for you have done that which is evil in the eyes of the Lord.

8. You have conspired against me and have taken that which is rightfully mine.

9. The agreement with Jacob Rose for the lease of my sawmill* has not been upheld.

10. Behold, I was <u>given for</u> my great sawmill only

*The sawmill was actually in Washoe Valley

one span of small indifferent mules, one aged worn-out harness, two yoke of oxen and an ancient wagon.

11. Behold, the true worth of my sawmill is 20 thousand talent of gold which must be rendered unto me.

12. Now, therefore, lodge not this night but gather together the money and have it delivered into my hands.

13. For if you do not proceed to do this work, behold, I know well that thou shalt surely be cursed.

14. Far be it, far be it from me that I should swallow up or destroy, but the hand of the Lord will be heavy upon you.

15. For the Lord will avenge us of our enemies.

16. Thou shalt be visited of the Lord of hosts with thunder, and with earthquake and great noise, with storm and tempest, and the flame of devouring fire.

17. And the two men who have directly sinned against me shall be living and dying symbols of God's displeasure in their persons, in their families and in their substances.

End of cable cord wood conveyor line where wood unloaded on ground was then re-loaded onto wagons. This operation was on Brockliss wood land near Mottsville. *(Courtesy of Nevada State Park Commission)*

Court in the Mott Barn

I N A BARN very like the one still standing on the August Kettenberg ranch, there was held in the middle of July 1856 a session of the United States District Court, presided over by Judge W.W. Drummond of the Third District of Utah Territory. The barn where the court was held was that of Hirman Mott, built in 1855. This was one of its first uses! Perhaps due to the environment or for some other reason, the Grand Jury chosen by Judge Drummond brought in no indictments.

It is said that complaints had been made concerning horse thieving, gambling, concubinage and other minor offenses committed along the Carson River Route. Rumor has it that the eighteen jurors, all gentiles, as the Mormons called non-Mormons, acknowledged among themselves that each had in some degree been guilty of these and other minor pioneer sins. The jurors neither condemned nor told on their neighbors, adopting the practice of other small societies and of primitive societies the world over. Judge Drummond, after nine days of futility, dismissed seven of the members and replaced them with Mormons. This act of purification produced two indictments, neither of which "stuck." The judge threatened to "iron" the grand jury but took no formal action. At the end of six weeks, the frustrated representative of the law departed, never to return again.

The barn reverted to its primary uses and the local residents to their customary activities — innkeeping, cattle raising and feeding, and country dances. How gay these were may be suggested by names the pioneers gave their dance halls: for example, in Mottsville it was the Tambourine and in Genoa, in 1853, the Amazon.

Barn on the Scossa Ranch. After the death of "Snowshoe" Thompson his widow married into the Scossa family. *(Courtesy of James A. Lawrence)*

The Hugh Park Barn now owned by August Kettenburg. Barns such as this and those following were the most conspicuous structures along the Carson River route. Barns dwarfed dwellings and were impressively related to the source of pioneer power — horse power. When there was a blacksmith shop nearby, the barn and shop became the service station of their time. The variety of roof styles suggests that there were several sources from which the builders took their designs. *(Courtesy of Juanita Schubert)*

The Israel Jones barn standing on the Carson River route where it is joined by the Mottsville Lane. *(Courtesy of Juanita Schubert)*

Detail of the Heitman barn showing the use of diagonal boards put together with hand wrought nails made on the forges of Henry Van Sickle. *(Courtesy of Juanita Schubert)*

David Brooks Park was born in Warwick County, Canada, on December 24, 1839, and died in Mottsville on July 17, 1908. He came to Mottsville in 1863. On May 17, 1870, Mr. Park took out his citizenship papers in Douglas County, State of Nevada. Throughout his life, he operated a ranch in Carson Valley and a large dairy each summer at Lake Tahoe. He was also active in county politics. He married Nevada Unity McCue on June 20, 1872. *(Courtesy of Brooks Park)*

Pioneer Banking

ON MAY 27, 1949, the *Record Courier* reported that Carson Valley was having the thrill of a modern day gold rush and it wasn't for nuggets or gold dust. Thus, in humorous vein, the local paper belatedly advised the citizens of the valley of a fact that had been a well-guarded secret from them for at least three weeks.

Turning back one page of history discloses that County Commissioner Melvin Schwake had somewhat earlier

Heinrick Frederick Dangberg was born in Halle (administrative district of Minden, Westphalia) Kingdom of Prussia, September 16, 1829 and died in Carson Valley on July 16, 1904. He came to the United States in 1848 and to Carson Valley in 1856. On February 16, 1863, he took out his citizenship papers in Douglas County, Territory of Nevada. On March 15, 1866, he married Margaret Gale Ferris. For the entire period of his residence in Carson Valley he was engaged in stock raising and agriculture. He served in the state assembly 1869-1873 and in the senate in 1879 and 1883-1885.

The Douglas County Farmers Bank in Gardnerville. *(Courtesy of Henry and Edna Frevert)*

bought the ranch owned in the 1850s by the Mott family and purchased in 1865 by David Brooks Park. On his newly acquired ranch Melvin began building a modern home on the site of the old Park house. In the course of the excavations the workmen on the job unearthed a number of gold coins; how many has never been determined to the satisfaction of any one. Suffice it to say that when the owner was finally advised of the "find," the workmen acknowledged that they had a few and the sheriff had a few "to keep until ownership was established." It has never been reported that the ownership problem was solved. In short, it was "finders keepers, losers weepers." This event was described in a feature story published in the *San Francisco Examiner* for October 9, 1949.

Again turning back several pages of history, we come upon the beginnings of banking in Carson Valley. David Brooks Park is known to have acted as banker for his neighbors up and down the West Fork of the Carson River. From the evidence of the coins retrieved, this service was performed until at least 1893, reported to be the date of the newest coin. During these years, Mr. Park had on hand sufficient money to accommodate his friends and neighbors in meeting taxes, payrolls, and in paying for the groceries or for grinding their wheat to make flour, to mention only a few of the needs for money.

This banking represented a practice paralleled on the East Fork by H.F. Dangberg who had two cast iron safes labeled on the inside door "Hall's Patent" and manufactured, it may be presumed, by Hall's Safe and Lock Company of Cincinnati, Ohio. These stood in his ranch home office. At times, tradition has it, they had stored in them as high as $50,000 in gold coin. One night when such funds were

in the safe, the women of the family, hearing prowlers gave the alarm. The men folk listened attentively and peered cautiously into the shadows to discover that an old cow, walking in her sleep, had wandered into the yard through an open gate!

Apparently Mr. Park had hidden some of his gold coins in a strong box in his basement for an emergency which never occurred. At long last the treasure was forgotten when the opening of the Douglas County Farmers Bank, in 1902, made personal banking services no longer necessary in Carson Valley. The bank was opened in Gardnerville by Arendt Jensen. Seven years later, on May 28, 1909, the Farmers Bank of Carson Valley which was founded by W.F. Dressler, H.F. Dangberg Land and Live Stock Company, Fritz Heise, C.M. Henningsen, D.W. Park (son of David Brooks Park) and others was opened in Minden.

Thrashers' Ball

THE THRASHING of grain, principally wheat, was one of the earliest agricultural activities along the Carson River Route. In 1857 or 1858, according to Henry Van Sickle, the Mott family of Mottsville had the first threshing machine. It was a poor machine and when a cylinder "busted," it killed one of the Motts.

Fortunately, other and better machines were put into operation in the following years. The thrashing machines were run by the men-folk of several valley families after the haying was over. On ranch after ranch men labored for long hours in the hot September air, polluted by the chaff and dust from the belching blowers. Nose, throat and eyes became irritated. In ranch kitchens, women, driven on by the desire to surpass their neighbors in serving tasty dinners and suppers to the men, stood over wood-burning stoves engulfed in steam and sweat and, sometimes, tears to achieve their end.

At long last, however, the labors of the hot summer months were over. It was a time for rejoicing, a time for gaiety, a time for love. And it was at such a time, in 1895, that young Willie Hansen rode his bicycle from the scene of thrashing to the home of Hugh Park where he asked if daughter Eliza could go with him that night to the Thrasher's Ball. Mr. Park called his fifteen-year-old daughter and the date was made. Willie returned two hours later in a buggy drawn by a high-stepping horse and they were off to the Raycraft's Exchange in Genoa. The thrashers were the hosts; the Raycrafts provided the supper and what a supper it was with everything home-grown and home-cooked. Lovely Eliza in her pink puff-plaited gown made for just such an occasion by her devoted aunt, Dr. Eliza Cook, danced until dawn with her future husband.

The Palmer Barn on the Indian Road Ranch

BEN PALMER (Parmer to his neighbors) was an early settler on the Carson River Route and a prominent member of the Carson Valley ranching community. A drover, he was often mentioned in the newspapers of the day. On August 17, 1875, the *Territorial Enterprise* reported that he drove 1,500 head of cattle from Seattle in Washington Territory to Carson Valley to be fed for the Virginia City butchers. Palmer purchased the cattle for $5.00 per head. It took three months to drive them to Carson Valley. Palmer was also a breeder of fine horses and introduced the Bonner Stock to Carson Valley.

Ben Palmer first came to Carson Valley in 1853. Later he returned to Missouri to bring his sister and her family

The Ben Palmer barn near Sheridan built in 1868 by Charles Holbrook. *(Courtesy of Juanita Schubert)*

Clarissa (Clarice) Church. *(Courtesy of Mildred Jepsen Clark)*

Eliza Cook, M.D.

C ARSON VALLEY'S proud claim to "firsts" in Nevada extends beyond the year of the first settlement to embrace the professional career of Eliza Cook who became the first woman doctor in Nevada. Born in Salt Lake City on February 5, 1856, Eliza came to Carson Valley with her family in 1870. They lived near Sheridan on the old Carson River Route. Here Eliza soon manifested an interest in the practice of medicine, lending aid to the local doctor, H. H. Smith of Genoa, who was so impressed with her talent for the care of the sick that he accepted her as an apprentice and then encouraged her to study medicine.

Eliza's parents came from England; the family was preceeded to Carson Valley by an uncle who soon after his arrival earned among the unlettered frontiersmen of the day the descriptive title of "Dictionary Cook." The polysyllabic words which he used may be considered advance notice that the Cook family had intellectual interest beyond those of the average settler. Inherited talent and family encouragement led the young Eliza to study medicine on her own. In 1884 at the age of 28, after two years of study — the usual period at that time — she received her M.D. degree from the Cooper College of Medicine in San Francisco.

After practicing for six years, Dr. Cook went to Philadelphia and New York City for a year of post-graduate study. Ten years later she went abroad to the British Isles, Europe, the Holy Land and Egypt. On her return she graciously gave many talks and lectures to the citizens of Carson Valley on the wonders of the Old World. To the amusement of Dr. Cook's relatives, her traveling companion told how Eliza, in Italy, had taken a naughty little boy across her knee and spanked him soundly.

Discipline and obedience were tenets of Eliza's faith. She was stern, but kindly. When called, often by a galloping horseman, to deliver a baby, she performed her professional duties as a doctor then returned each day afterward for two weeks to bathe the baby and care for the mother. And, if the head of the house was a kind and thoughtful husband and father, she would also help to keep the family going by performing more menial tasks in the household.

The drives through the valley to the widely separated homes of her patients were made in a top buggy to which she herself hitched one of her own horses. She answered calls to places as far away as Markleeville, California. If she returned after dark, in the days before flashlights, she knew the time on her way home by whether or not the lights were still shining in successive ranch houses.

Eliza set broken limbs, making her own splints; she had a beautiful little apothecary's scale and with it she measured her own powders to the delight of her little great niece who stood by wide-eyed while the delicate operation was in progress. Members of the family contributed to the suc-

to live with him. Palmer and his sister, as the story goes, had bought their way out of slavery; the sister was married to a white man named Barber. Her oldest child by a former marriage was Clarissa Church; the other four or five children were Barbers. They and their neighbors were on very friendly terms; the Palmer-Barber family were famous for their hospitality and for their charity. They always had flour, or even money, for the poor or afflicted.

And like all ranches along the Carson River Route, the Palmer-Barber ranch was also a wayside inn. On Christmas night, in 1859, it had as guests a young couple, August Dangberg (brother of H.F. Dangberg) and his wife, who were completing the last lap of a four-month journey from Prussia to Carson Valley. To the young girl who watched with mixed emotions the little black faces with their startlingly white eyeballs pressed against the balusters of the stairway, it was indeed a new and strange world to which she had come. She was, however, equal to the challenges of the new world — to this one and to many others as she demonstrated when she converted her brother-in-law's old gold washing pan into a colander!

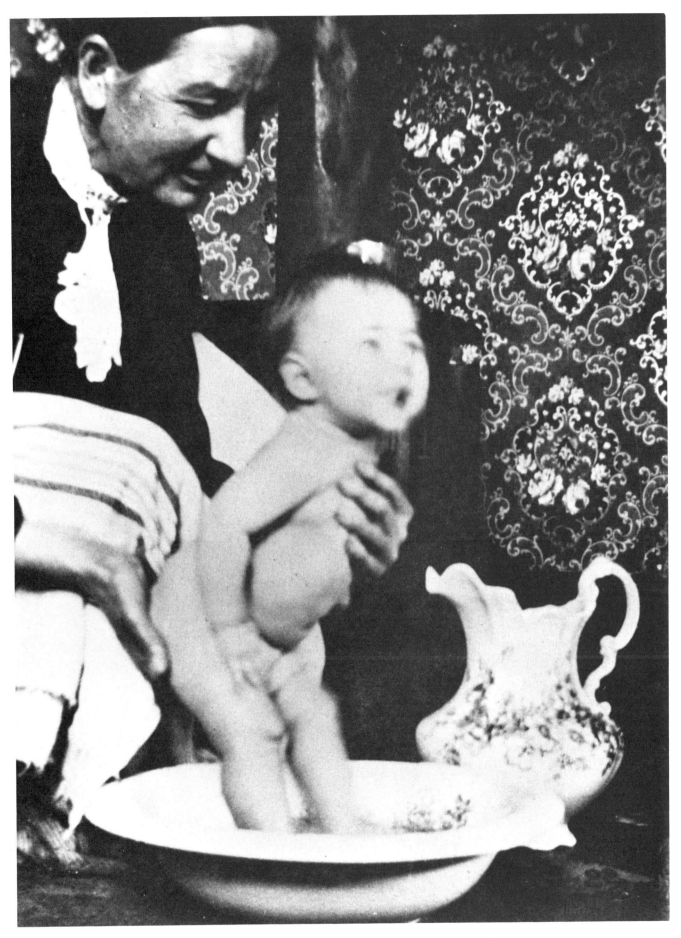

Dr. Eliza Cook with one of her babies. *(Courtesy of Mrs. Eliza Park Hansen)*

cess of this home-operated pharmacy by saving all their tissue paper. These sheets were carefully sterilized with dry heat and cut into uniform size for dispensing pulverized medication, or powders, as they were then called.

In fair weather or foul, this courageous little woman ventured forth. Floods did not deter her, though the river had to be forded when bridges were washed out, nor did frost stay her even when icicles hung from the steaming nose and mouth of her horse.

In contrast to this strength and hardiness was her talent for the gentler arts of homemaking. From the cool pantry in her home near Mottsville came the fragrance of stored apples and preserves; from her kitchen, the aroma of freshly baked bread and, in her dining room, she served the most delicious lunches of ham, baked beans and applesauce. She

also crocheted in patterns of her own design, such as a baby cap of wild roses. She made exquisite lace and tatting. And last, but not least, she cultivated a lovely flower garden where foxgloves, lilies and violets grew.

Eliza's home was filled with books on an astonishing number of subjects. Her interest in education was widely recognized.

The philosophic calm of her outlook on life was demonstrated when she was found one morning in her ninety-first year in her home in bed. The beautiful and customary order of her household and the position of her hands folded across her bosom told that she may have known upon retiring that this was to be her last sleep. She was smiling.

Eliza Cook, M.D., throughout her long life was a lover of learning and dedicated to her profession.

Dr. Cook standing in the door of her home near Mottsville. *(Courtesy of Anna Neddenriep Dressler)*

Sheridan

IN THE YEARS following 1851, the stations along the Carson River Route were beautified by the planting of yellow rose bushes and Lombardy poplars, dear to the hearts of the Mormon settlers. By 1860 one of these stations started by Moses Job in the early 1850s had become the village of Sheridan. Moses Job sold his store and the 800 acres on which the village stood to J. W. Haines and I. W. Duncan in 1861. We are afforded a picture of the merchandizing of a pioneer store in the letter of a clerk in the employ of Mr. Duncan and Mr. Billis. At the time of the writing — October 31, 1865 — Mr. Billis had gone to San Francisco where he had purchased 9000 pounds of supplies, exclusive of flour, for his winter customers. The young clerk, Isaac Des Isles, wrote to his family in Maine:

"Last Sunday sold over $200.00 dollars worth for cash. I would like tending store much better if did not have to do business on Sunday but on that day we have more to do than any other day of the week. The more I see of Sunday's labor the more I think it wrong. It may prosper for a short time but I am of the opinion that it is the reason why so many lose so much here in Speculation, but they think because they are with the Romans they must do as they do, but in some respects I cannot nor will not do as they. Some of them call me a Deacon because I will not Gamble or even play cards on Sunday for amusement with the exception of tending Store on Sunday I conduct myself the same as at Home. It seems to me as though some think because they was in Cal they can do as they like & no one to molest them, but I can say it is not so with me, & I often think only for my Parents good advice I might have been a drunken worthless wrech. I often think when I see a man & his sons up to a Bar what an example that is to set before his children, but enough of this at present. The weather has been very pleasant for some days past, but quite Cool, on the Mountains there has been several spirts of Snow, have not had any Rain of any amount since April, much different than the States the

The Sheridan Hotel about 1890. In the surrey are members of the Brockliss family: Arthur, Emma, Duane (Tucke) and Raymond. In 1888 Sheridan had one store, two hotels, a post office, a saloon and a blacksmith and wagon shop. The surveyor general in his report of 1889-90 said that Sheridan was the metropolis of the West Fork. *(Courtesy of Francis Brockliss Lampe and Margie Johnson Springmeyer)*

The Sheridan blacksmith shop before 1909. *(Courtesy of Anna Neddenriep Dressler)*

The Sheridan Bar about 1900. Behind the bar are Arthur and Bill Brockliss; in front are Arthur Park and John Brockliss. *(Courtesy of the Nevada State Park Commission)*

The Sheridan General Merchandise store of Barrett and Tucke about 1900. Above the store was the dance hall. *(Courtesy of the Nevada State Park Commission)*

Ranchmen stack their Grain in the Fields then wait for the Thrashers to come & thrash it out, seldom think of Rain. While Mr. Billis was below I had him to purchase a set of Tomb Stones for dear Bro Chesnel, they will be over soon I have given up the idea of getting an iron Railing as they are about to enclose the Burying Yard (the Mottsville Cemetery), and as the Community will make that their Burying Ground they will keep the Fence in Repair.''

The blacksmith shop in Sheridan was one of a number of the same genre which dotted the road in the great days of twenty-four horse teams, hauling freight wagons with back actions attached. These were the trucks and trailers of the time. Along with the inns and saloons, blacksmith shops with their busy anvils were the first businesses set up at intervals along the emigrant trail. Hauling was at its peak when the mines flourished on the Comstock and in Bodie as well as lesser centers in Alpine County. During these years the blacksmith shops provided employment for a number of men. The son of one of these employees whose family comprised four sons and six daughters tells how hard life in Carson Valley could be in the 1870s for the

family of a man who would support ten children by shoeing horses and fitting iron tires on wagon wheels (adapted from a letter, courtesy of Harold Park):

"We were extremely poor. Mother did all her cooking in a big iron pot in a rock fireplace. One of my earliest recollections is going with her to scrape up alkali to mix with her sour dough to make bread.

"On my seventh birthday my mother made me a marvelous cake and how good it tasted. She made seven little flat cakes like hot cakes and stuck them together with honey! My playmate was an Indian boy, Tulymahu; he was a good companion, I envied him his good clothing and bow and arrows. His clothes were made of nicely tanned buckskin. He had a real good bow and could shoot it well, while I had one made from willow and could not shoot it nearly so well. Mother made her cloth on the spinning wheel and was handy with knitting needles. My bed was a pile of corn husks in the corner of the cabin and I slept with a buffalo skin under me and one over me. My clothing was tanned buffalo skins with the hair on; pants, coat and moccasins. Why someone did not shoot me for a wild animal I will never know.''

Pioneers of Carson Valley about 1869. Lute Olds (one of the "border ruffians") is seated the first on the left.

Carson Valley's Haunted Barn

ABOUT TWELVE miles south of Genoa, according to W.F. Skyhawk *(Pony Express Historical Series* — No. 22), stands the haunted barn of Fairview, built over a cellar that once was part of the old Cotton Hotel, another hostelry on the Carson River Route. It was here that a miner named Sawtooth was murdered for the gold that filled his pockets. The border ruffians who killed him then buried him beneath potato sacks in the cellar. In 1861, Sam Brown, who had killed twelve men and was after his "baker's dozen" — number thirteen — was killed across the road at the barn of Lute Olds. Before burial at Genoa, Sam was placed temporarily in the cellar where folks claim that spirits of Brown and Sawtooth heave potatoes nightly and shake the rafters. Old timers also say that Sawtooth was the only man who ever found Snowshoe Thompson's lost mine although hundreds have hunted for it. "Ghosts are still there today," said old timer Fritz Dressler who says he was once heaved across the cellar.

W. F. Skyhawk celebrates these events in verse:

Down came robbers from the canyon!
　Down from Border Ruffian Range!
Stealthy slinkers in the darkness!
　Hear the story weird and strange:
Came the horse thief gang one evening
　As the clock struck midnight hour;
Blazed their guns that killed old Sawtooth
　Close beside his water tower.

Looted they and silent laid him
　Shrouded 'neath potato sacks.
Thence came Sam Brown's ghost to join him,
　And they run but leave no tracks.
Phantoms romp, and nightly frolic,
　Till Old Sol proclaims the dawn,
Spirits shake the eerie rafters
　Sockety-eyed, and faces wan.

Ghosts of Sam Brown, and of Sawtooth,
　In that haunted cellar rule.
Venture not lest you inflame them!
　Be not kindred to a fool!
Fairview's barn is gruesome haunted,
　And forever is its doom.
Where the ghosts heave big potatoes
　One heaved Dressler 'cross the room.

Fairview

THIS QUIET country schoolhouse stood until recently at a place associated with crime and punishment in the busy days along the Carson River Route. During the years between 1857, when the Mormon settlers were called back to Salt Lake, and July 11, 1861, when the territorial government was set up, the valley found itself in a grave situation, described by "Tennessee" in the June 29, 1859 issue of the *San Francisco Herald:* "Numerous thieves and murderers run loose here, and we have no tribunal before which their guilt can be proven. The organic act allows no criminal jurisdiction to Probate or County Courts, and the Mormon Legislative Assembly (in Salt Lake City) refuses to make any appropriations for sustaining the Federal judiciary in attending to territorial business."

The Fairview School, originally situated about a mile north of where it stood in the 1890s, was just north of the ranch and hostelry of "Lucky Bill" Thorington who was hanged on June 19, 1858, for harboring a murderer. It was a bare half mile from the barn from which Henry Van Sickle on July 6, 1861, acting courageously in the absence of courts of law to protect himself and others, shot the notorious murderer and desperado Sam Brown. And finally it was near the hostelry of the Olds brothers whose colorful activities are described in the verse on page 66 which gave the name of Horse Thief Meadow to the grassy vale westward over the crest of the Sierra Nevada. It was reported in the *San Francisco Herald,* issue of September 7, 1856, that stolen horses were being herded in a small valley near Carson Valley. Three men were engaged in this enterprise, one of whom, George Howard, had been arrested earlier in Placerville for horse stealing. He was captured by a party of immigrants.

In contrast to these happenings was the life led, for a brief period — October 1858 to September 1865 — by Ira M. Luther, an emigrant from New York. Luther and

The Fairview School about 1895. It was built about 1890 to replace an earlier school situated in Luther Canyon. Trees were planted around the new school by such boys as Ernie Fay and Bill Settelmeyer, each lad taking responsibility for watering his tree. Later these helpful lads joined their playmates to chase the teacher's buggy horse all over the valley. They finally caught it and returned the horse to Miss Mary Lloyd just as school was closing! Ernie Fay, first on the left, and Bill Settelmeyer, fourth in the front row. *(Courtesy of Fred H. and Irma Settelmeyer)*

. . . and the trees grew.

D. R. Jones who came to Carson Valley in 1853.
(Courtesy of Nevada State Historical Society)

his family lived at the mouth of the canyon which for many years bore his name and is shown on recent maps as Fay Canyon. Here Luther built a sawmill and also erected, on a foundation of cottonwood limbs, a spacious — for those days — house with French windows which looked out across Carson Valley on the pastel-tinted Pine Nut Range. Attached to the house was a milk cellar through which the cool and sparkling waters of the canyon creek ran. The house is now the home of Ernest and Emma Dressler.

These seven years were filled with grueling toil for both Mr. and Mrs. Luther who were unaccustomed to ranch work. They were also years of anxiety. In 1860, as history tells us, there was trouble with the Indians. How serious this trouble was is reflected in the testimony of D.R. Jones (Anderson vs. Bassman, Plaintiff's Testimony, pp. 367-368). He says that everyone was fleeing the country in fear, and that he and his wife, both very young, would leave their house at night and hide in the brush lest the Indians set fire to the grass and burn them while they slept.

One night Indians surrounded the house while Mrs. Luther, who was soon after to be taken to Virginia City where her daughter was born on August 17, lay trembling in the dark expecting an attack. On another night a brave entered the house and surprised Mr. Luther who was reading. With his revolver in hand, Mr. Luther reached behind the stove and shot the intruder to protect himself. Was the Indian killed? In his account of the incident, Mr. Luther does not say.

Interior of the Fairview School in 1898. The future Senator Settelmeyer, then age six, is seated in the third row on the right. *Courtesy of Fred H. and Irma Settelmeyer)*

In later years, the Luther children recalled the joys of life when they and the children of other settlers attended the progenitor of the Fairview School. Here, Homer Luther, toeing a crack in the floor, learned to recite: "Breathes there a man with soul so dead who never to himself hath said, this is my own, my native land?" He and the other children went picking buffalo berries in the canyon in the summer. In winter they appropriated the jaw bones of oxen to slide down the slopes on the snow!

The Fairview School

T HE SECOND Fairview schoolhouse was abandoned in 1929 when, in the name of progress, the district schools of Douglas County were consolidated. Residents of Carson Valley fondly remember this schoolhouse as the scene of more than one exercise that had nothing to do with the processes of public school education. Instead, it was somewhat startlingly associated with a subsidiary or secondary use of schoolhouses in the early days. This secondary use had to do with the holding of church serv-

ices, dear to the hearts of pioneer women, but often inspiring their less pious husbands and brothers to perpetrate pranks.

Ernie Fay tells of an occasion when his father was one of these perpetrators. Mr. Daley, the Mormon preacher, was going to hold services in the evening in the schoolhouse and, as everyone in the neighborhood planned to attend, it was a perfect set-up for a demonstration. During the day, Ernie's father and uncle both went up into the attic and filled the school bell full of shot, securing it with a string which extended down to their seats in the schoolroom.

As the congregation assembled that evening, venerable pioneer D.R. Jones, one of the staunch churchmen of the community who had for twenty-five years been an Elder in the Church of Jesus Christ of Latter-day Saints in Carson Valley, arose each time anyone wanted to sit in his row and allowed the person to pass, retaining the outside seat for himself. Mr. Daley began his exhortation to sinners and as he progressed to the climax with a mighty peroration, a thunderous clap was heard above — Ernie's father had pulled the string attached to the bell. Mr. Daley, undaunted, leaped up holding his hands aloft and exclaimed, "Well, that's good luck." The congregation turned to look reproachfully at the innocent Mr. Jones.

Susie. *(Courtesy of Juanita Schubert)*

Murder

THE LINES OF that rugged, mischievous old face were not all put there by the emotions of love and pride. Many of them were the scars of battle — battles of wit and of murderous anger.

About 1895 Susie was living or tarrying with a group of Indians, kinfolk of one degree or another, at the mouth of Luther Canyon where they were working on the old Luther ranch then owned by Sprague and presently the property of Ernie Dressler and his son Bud.

One evening in the darkening shadows of the Sierra, an Indian named Jack rode up to the camp, jumped off his horse and tied it to a sage bush. Jack had a rifle. He started up the hill, unnoticed by the group when suddenly a shot rang out in the clear air; a woman was hit and killed by Jack's rifle shot. Then he shot a man by the name of Jim who fell to the ground, mortally wounded. Jack was reloading when the shell stuck in the gun. At this moment a man named Jerry ran up behind Jack, grabbed his arms and held them while a woman grabbed the gun from his hands and hit Jack over the head; Jack fell to the ground. Then Susie ran, got a big rock and just stood over Jack and hammered his head to jelly. Prompted by a belated sense of decency or in obedience to tribal custom, Susie then covered Jack's head with sand.

It was later that Mike Fay, a nearby rancher, who was summoned to the scene of carnage by another woman, learned the reason for the killing: Jim had stolen Jack's woman. Justice had been swift and final. Jim and his paramour were dead; the avenging husband had been destroyed. Peace and quiet were restored.

One morning six months later an old squaw came to the Fay ranch and asked to see the gun that killed Jim. She said, "Jack, he kill my boy. Me gottum no boy killum jackrabbits, makum blankets, me gottum no boy gettum pinenuts. God damn Jack." Mrs. Fay gave her the gun and breakfast.

Humane Responses in the Stone Age

REACTIONS OF the Washoe to crime are unbelievably swift as we have seen. Reactions to sufferings of beasts are of a different tempo as shown in the accounts that follow:

One day an Indian was seen standing near a horse that had rolled over into a ditch where, lying on its back, it could not get up. Mr. Fay, passing by, stopped to observe the situation. "Why don't you turn the horse over so he can get on his feet?" he asked the Washoe. "Oh," said the Washoe, "Him not my horse."

Another time the Washoes were gathered back of the Fay house for a dance. Most of them came on horseback. Mr. Fay always let them turn their horses out to feed at the well-filled hay racks. One Indian came and tied his horse to a sage bush. Mr. Fay thought this strange and after two days asked the Indian why he didn't take his horse in the corral where he could eat. "Oh," said the Washoe, "Him gottum plenty eat last summer."

HAPPENINGS ON THE CARSON RIVER

The Conversion of Monroe

ON PIONEER ranches along the Carson River, oxen were the chief source of power. According to reminiscing Owen Jones, son of Mormon Elder D.R. Jones, an ox driver's stock in trade was his powerful, commanding voice. It could not be developed; a man had to be born with it and when a team of oxen heard such a voice they would get right into the yoke and dig. These drivers often earned as much as ten dollars a day. Such a one was George Monroe who had a powerful vocabulary of profanity and a voice that could be heard for a mile on a cold, frosty morning. The story goes that two Mormon missionaries came into the valley from Salt Lake City looking for converts to their church. They held their services in the original Fairview schoolhouse. Some of the more religiously inclined residents persuaded them to have Monroe join their church and, consequently, they hoped to mend his ways in the use of free and easy profanity.

The missionaries were young, ambitious, and anxious to accomplish some real achievement for their cause and, understandably, to place some "feathers in their own caps." They promised to use their best efforts to convert Monroe. In due course they were pleased to announce to their congregation that they had finally succeeded after a lot of hard work and argument. All were told to be at a certain place on the river early the following Sunday morning to witness the solemn baptismal service.

When the time came, there were quite a few of the residents present. It was in the fall of the year on a very cold and frosty morning. The water itself was bitter cold. The missionaries said that was what they desired — the colder the water the better so the convert would never forget his obligations. Monroe was very tall, a giant in stature, and had the strength of an ox. The missionaries were medium-sized men. They decided to take no chances so they both waded out into the stream, one on each side of Monroe. They immersed him deep into the icy water and when they raised him up, Monroe yelled, at the top of his voice, the most profane oaths. The missionaries promptly immersed him again and, this time, held him down as long as they dared without drowning him. When they finally let him up, he walked out as meek as a lamb.

Everyone congratulated the young men on the good work they had done. All sat down to a hearty breakfast served at a farm house nearby. Everyone was happy to think that the "most wicked man" in the valley had been converted. That same night, Monroe met some of his cronies at a saloon not far distant and went on a spree. The next day when he went back to his work driving ox teams he could be heard swearing as loud and long as before. The missionaries gave him up as a "hard nut to crack" and departed for Salt Lake City "sadder but wiser men."

The baptism of Monroe no doubt took place near the bridge on Nevada State Route 88 over the West Fork slough at the Squires Ranch of early days. This was, in the memory of Ernie Fay, a usual spot during his boyhood in the 1890's, for the practice of these rites by the Mormon preachers. Here it was that another incident of doubtful solemnity occurred when three ladies of the community were scheduled to be immersed. Two of them, with admirable foresight, sewed weights in the hems of their long white baptismal robes. The third, no doubt concentrating more on the spiritual aspects of the rite than the practical, did not take this precaution. When she stepped into the river the hem of her robe floated on the surface of the water to the dismay of her frantic spouse who stood nearby calling helplessly, "Liz, Liz, pull down your skirt!"

Oxen

F ROM THE DAYS of the immigrants to the end of the Nineteenth century, oxen were used on the ranches of Carson Valley.

Much of the heavy teaming and farm work in the early days was done by oxen. Owen Jones, son of pioneer D.R. Jones, gives an account of the uses of oxen. The average distance travelled by a heavily loaded ox team was about five miles a day. An acre of new land turned over by a team of three yoke of oxen and two men in one day was a very good day's work. It required very heavy motive power to turn over this heavily sodded land; the ox teams were the only available power. Strange as it may seem, it required good sound judgment and business ability to operate a string of ox teams, just as it does nowadays to operate a line of trucks.

All of these oxen had to be what was then called "salted" — thoroughly salted — before they could be put to hard work. The method of doing this was to put the oxen in a corral and feed them dry feed along with all the salt and water that they would take for at least two weeks before putting them to hard work. It was not safe to take animals off green grass and put them to work without conditioning them beforehand. A disease called "red water" and another disease called "lung fever" (pneumonia) were both very prevalent among the oxen. They had to be vaccinated and inoculated against these afflictions. The method used in vaccinating an animal was to cut a very small incision in the dulap, under the neck, and place a small portion of asafetida into this opening, under the skin, and sew it up. The method of inoculating against lung fever, was to cut a small incision into the animal's tail, and place in it a small piece of flesh from an animal that had recently died from this disease, bind it up very tightly, and within a day or two, the animal would become slightly ill. After it had fully recovered from this slight sickness, the end of the tail was cut off. This act was believed to immunize the animal. Whether this had any merit or not, Mr. Jones was not able to say. The practice, however, accounted for so many early day work oxen with bobtails. It seemed cruel, but it was far better to lose the tail than the ox.

Another use for oxen not noted by Mr. Jones was for ferrying. When the East Fork of the Carson River was high, Mr. Wheeler who lived on the stream near the Twelve Mile House rented the services of his ox to foot travelers who would board the ox and for one dollar be transported safely across the raging waters.

The court records of Douglas County provide some pen portraits of oxen. Thus on July 29 of 1868, H.F. Dangberg sued William Foster to recover the following:

1 bob-tailed red ox with white spots
1 red ox with one droop horn
1 red ox with small dirty white spots
1 black ox with white spots with one horn partly off
1 dark brown ox
1 spotted or mixed red ox

Above reasonably worth $600.

German Weddings

I T WAS TEN years or more after the disuse of the southernmost length of the Carson River Route, before this neglected segment of it came again into the orbit of activity in Carson Valley. In 1870 and after, this upper end of Carson Valley appeared in quite different dress. It was no longer supported by teamster and teams and wagons on their way to and from California. It had become an area of settlement for men operating ranches. These men were, for the most part, Germans who had come from the Old Country in 1870 and after. The timber land around the village of Fredericksburg was the center of their activity. Here the large clan of Neddenrieps from Hanover, Germany were the principal settlers.

German love of fun and frolic survived in this new world settlement. It persisted over long periods in spite of hard work and hardships. Social life centered on weddings (and what weddings they were!) giving expression to all the pent-up desires for merry-making of the small German community. First of these of note was that of Henry Bassman, whose mother was a Neddenriep to Mary Elges in 1875. The second was that of Fritz Heise to Dorothea Neddenriep in 1886; the third was that of Charley Springmeyer to Theresa Neddenriep in 1895 and the fourth, that of F.W. Stodieck to Adele Bassman, daughter of Henry Bassman in 1899. Finally, there was the wedding of Henry Tucke and Emma Bruns — Emma's mother was also a Neddenriep.

Dorothea was the first of a number of beautiful Neddenriep girls to be married in Fredericksburg. She was the daughter of Claus and the sister of Henry, who had eight lovely daughters of his own. By the time all eight of them had married, Neddenrieps became the connective tissue linking many valley families, German as well as others, in a widespread kinship system.

It was at Dorothea's wedding on a Saturday that one of the guests practiced the legerdemain with the clock that has become a legend in Carson Valley. His wife, a strict Presbyterian in the observance of Sunday as a day of worship, was also a devotee of the dance. In order that she might enjoy herself to the full, the hands of the clock were mysteriously moved back to an earlier hour each time they approached midnight; thus, she was permitted unwittingly, but nevertheless wickedly, to indulge her passion until the early hours of dawn on Sunday. Did grandmother inflict some form of punishment on grandfather for this deceit? This has not been recorded but grandmother always blushed when she told this story.

Of the next of these celebrations we have elaborate

The bride and groom: Frederick William Stodieck and Adele Bassman. *(Courtesy of Elvin and William Stodieck)*

Guests at the Stodieck-Bassman wedding grouped in front of the stone root cellar. Papa Starke and his organ are framed in the window above. *(Courtesy of Elvin and William Stodieck)*

74

Guests at the Tucke-Bruns wedding. *(Courtesy of Anna Heise)*

accounts written by newsmen who indulged their taste for extravagant literary expression and, it may be surmised, for Gargantuan pleasures as well.

In 1895 when the golden wedding of the bride's grandparents, Mr. and Mrs. Claus Neddenriep, was celebrated on the same date as her marriage, the delighted reporter noted that everybody — all of the 250 guests — followed suit when the Reverend George R. Davis of the Protestant Episcopal Church of Carson City, on completion of the ceremony, kissed the lovely bride, Theresa Neddenriep, the belle of Fredericksburg. Ah, Charley Springmeyer, all conceded, was a lucky man! And grandfather saw the same enthusiastic bussing technique applied to his bride of fifty years after the Reverend Mr. Becker, the Lutheran minister of Carson Valley re-united the elderly couple.

Dancing? Indeed. They tripped "the light fantastic" on the floor laid for the occasion in the barn, built in 1880, across from grandfather's home. At length hungry and breathless they dashed back to the house for viands prepared by three relays of cooks — choice parts of several beef, pork by the hundredweight, chickens, ducks, turkeys, cakes as large as a moon and three feet high, beer in kegs, claret by the case, port in casques, headcheese, stuffed goose — and, in spite of this, or because of it, they danced and dined all Sunday afternoon and until daylight Monday morning.

For the Stodieck-Bassman wedding on June 2, 1899, invitations were sent to sixty German families in Carson Valley. Fifty-eight came. The absent ones were prevented by the untimely arrival of the stork in their homes. The bride was tall and graceful, beautifully attired. Her gown was silk the hue of ashes of roses trimmed with passementerie and applique. The bridesmaids, sister Ida and friend Genie Arnot, were gowned in white. A floor for dancing had been laid in the barn. In the stone root cellar, the tables were spread for the wedding dinner. No expense, by order of the bride's father, had been spared. Here Mr. Beggs dispensed Fredericksburg beer, fine wines and also temperance beverages as well as endless varieties of cigars.

For two weeks before the wedding, Papa Starke, an organ grinder and sometime cook, had been preparing for the feast — pies, cakes, etc. — under the stipulation that, in no circumstances, was he to get drunk until the festivities were over. Papa obeyed.

The ceremony was celebrated by his Honor, Judge N.D. Arnot of Alpine County, who for many years in the absence of clergymen in Carson Valley had performed this community service. It is reported that he used the beautiful Episcopal ceremony "improvised for the occasion." And what was that improvisation? No record remains other than the statement that the young couple were united by double rings whereupon "in his happy style" the Judge pronounced them man and wife. Dining and dancing to the strains of C.M. Taylor's fiddle followed all the rest of the day and throughout the night.

At long last it was all over and, "Ach, du lieber Augustine," Papa got gloriously drunk.

75

'Snowshoe' Thompson

IF SETTLERS along the Carson River Route could have chosen a man as a symbol to represent qualities on which they prided themselves, the choice would undoubtedly have fallen on John A. Thompson who, in the inexact nomenclature of the day, bore the sobriquet "Snowshoe." This man came from Placerville to Genoa for the first time in January 1856. He came the ninety miles across the snow-covered Sierra Nevada on skis to carry the mail. On this trip and the many others he made during 1856 and the years following, he became enamored of Carson Valley and also of English-born Agnes Singleton of Sheridan. In 1866 they were married and settled in Diamond Valley where "Snowshoe" lived until his death from pneumonia in 1876.

In Diamond Valley his memory is preserved in the names of several ditches which he built to carry water from the West Fork of the Carson to his land. It was here that his only son was born and learned to ski on miniature skis carved by "Snowshoe." And to this ranch home he addressed two letters to his wife when he was in the nation's capitol in 1872, instructing her to have the spring plowing done on the dry land and to have it sown. In preparation for this, she was to have the boys — the contemporary way of speaking of hired men — take the red plow to Genoa and "get it fixed in good order." This was the "Snowshoe" Thompson known to pioneers of Carson Valley.

The two letters — now the treasured possessions of Miss Lillian Bergevin of Minden — were written when Mr. Thompson was in Washington, D.C. to present his case to Congress for a modest $6000, representing compensation for carrying the mail from Sacramento to settlements east of the Sierra Nevada. After 1857, this service was performed without contract.

"Snowshoe" Thompson and his son. *(Courtesy of Lillian Bergevin)*

The house "Snowshoe" Thompson built when he was married. *(Courtesy of Lillian Bergevin)*

The building on the left is the first home of "Snowshoe" Thompson in Diamond Valley; it was a dugout. *(Courtesy of Lillian Bergevin)*

How important this mail was to business men and to immigrants from foreign shores living east of the Sierra Nevada is indicated in the reports of newsmen in Sacramento Valley who, from time to time, noted that Mr. Thompson was extending the length of his regular crossing time (five days) while waiting for the arrival of the Atlantic mail which at that time came to California by boat. Thompson and his friends expected that he would one day be compensated for this valuable service. The failure of his petition to Congress is a sad but not unfamiliar commentary on rewards for selfless service.

Monetary rewards? *No!* but in the hall of fame, this son of Norway becomes ever more honored and appreciated as the years roll by. Jack Schaefer (1965) writes of Thompson's "unmatched strength" as indestructible as his mountains. Don Ashbaugh (1963) writes of the "astonishing" "Snowshoe" Thompson, and Francis P. Farquhar (1965) says, "Thompson remains the unrivaled champion of some of the toughest phases of the art of skiing."

Perhaps the most glowing expression of admiration has come from the pen of an officer of the Marines, W.F. Skyhawk in articles appearing in the *Pony Express Courier* (Placerville) in a number of issues in 1941 and 1942. Here Thompson is called "hero without parallel, flying eagle of the roaring fifties, the bird-man of the Wild West, courageous and unafraid." The enthusiastic author then proceeds with carefree disregard of dates and records to connect Thompson, one after another, with the names of prominent settlers in Carson Valley. Perhaps the most penetrating appraisal is that of Angel (1881) stating that Thompson possessed "fortitude of mind and spirit." The judgment of him by his contemporaries in Carson Valley in a similar sober vein was that "Snowshoe" Thompson was an energetic man and a leader in enterprise.

Log and Wood Drives

F LOATING LOGS and driving wood down the East Fork of the Carson was permitted by an act of the Territorial Legislature of Nevada approved November 21, 1861. It was an act authorizing and empowering C.H. Hobbes, J.C. Russell, David Smith, and J.C. Pennell to improve the East Fork of the Carson River from where it crossed the California line to Empire City below Carson City by removing logs, rocks, opening sloughs and cleaning out other obstructions to make the river suitable for the purpose of rafting logs down for manufacture into lumber and other timber. The act was amended December 10, 1862 to include, in addition to logs, timber of all kinds for a period of five years.

After March 1, 1862, the ranchers of Carson Valley found that they had to cope with something that had no bearing on raising hay. Although the woodmen boomed the sloughs and dammed the ditches to keep the saw logs, measuring three to three and a half feet in diameter, from

leaving the main channel, the wood, being of lesser thickness and shorter length, floated into the sloughs and clogged them so that the water flowed over the fields, spreading trash, bark and sand. On one occasion this caused a log jam above the Boyd Bridge that was so serious it had to be blown up with black powder. More damaging to the ranchers, however, were the woodmen — the wood drivers themselves — who trampled down the grass — grass that when cut for hay could in certain circumstances bring as much as $100 or even $400 per ton!

This unexpected intrusion into the world of raising hay and grain and feeding livestock created mixed reactions: Mandelbaum and Klauber, the Genoa merchants who also had one of the largest ranches on the East Fork, sued the woodmen for damages to their property; H.F. Dangberg saw it as an opportunity to have the channel of the East Fork through his ranch cleaned and straightened; others accepted payment for damages or claimed the logs that floated into their ditches.

When clearing the channel, the woodmen cut the willows instead of grubbing them. On Dangberg's property this resulted in the logs tearing into the banks as the willow roots rotted. Serious damage to the banks was repaired by building levees strong enough to keep the waters in the channel and thus preventing overflow through sloughs and the swamping of the land. In consequence, Dangberg averred the woodmen did him some good.

The floating of logs from the forests of Alpine County, forty miles to the south of Carson Valley, continued to supply the large steam-powered sawmill at Empire City until, according to Mr. Russell, the logs had to be hauled off distant slopes to streams where the water was sufficient to float them. In these circumstances it proved to be cheaper to get the logs in Washoe Valley. This was in 1866. However, the driving of wood from Alpine County forests continued. From 1873 until in the nineties, the chief wood driver was Sam Longabaugh, one time recorder of Douglas County.

The Surveyor General of Nevada in his *Report* for 1889-1890 states that a compilation from incomplete reports furnished for the past 30 years showed that 350,000,000 feet of timber was floated down the Carson as were 500,000 cords of wood. During these years, several flumes, also carrying logs to the Carson, were in operation on the east slope of the Sierra Nevada in Carson Valley.

The drama that these wood drives afforded the communities along the river was savored by the pens of the Genoa pressmen. Every year about March they noted preparations for the great event. Thus on a day in March 1877, a twenty-four horse team hitched to a wagon loaded with one of the large river boats and twelve men to work on the drive passed through town. Despite this early start, or perhaps owing to it, 7,000 cords missed the main drive. On July 10, these were hung up and dragged down the river by sixty men using pickaroons. The editor was skeptical of the drive ever getting through Carson Valley where, at this time of year, all the water was being diverted for irrigation. Failure to get through to Empire would entail great financial loss to the owners, he said.

The following year further hazards of rafting of logs,

Boat carrying gear of wood drivers who stand about with their picaroons. *(Courtesy of Douglas Ford)*

Wood drive on the East Fork of the Carson. Holding the wood at Young's Crossing, waiting for a head of water that would permit floating it through Carson Valley. *(Courtesy of Nevada State Museum)*

firewood, and lumber were chronicled when one of the men, assisting in breaking a log-jam, lost his balance above the Carson Falls in Alpine County and disappeared beneath the moving cord wood. His hat and glove were all that survived the grinding of three hundred cords of wood as they went over the brink.

In contrast to this grim event, many were the gallons of whiskey drunk with gusto by the agile woodmen who rode the logs downstream. In this way were they compensated for frequent duckings in the icy waters and an occasional broken limb.

A. C. Pratt, editor and publisher of the *Carson Valley News,* inspired by the annual spectacular, thought up another use for the limited waters of the Carson. In March of 1877, Pratt, together with R.E. Montgomery and others, calling themselves the "Genoa Slack Water Navigation Company," built a boat christened the "Amelia" to be launched on the Carson for fishing, hunting and pleasure "within the extremities" of Carson Valley. Two years later, in the March "freshet" of that year, the "Amelia" was washed three miles down the river before it was rescued and presumably ended its "slack water" career. A.C. Pratt whose dream child it was, soon after sold *The Carson Valley News.* The "Amelia" was not heard of again.

Water, Water, Who's Got the Water!

THE SPARKLING waters of the Carson, the quietly flowing irrigation ditches, the calm-surfaced sloughs and reservoirs with flocks of waterfowl flying overhead give no hint of the battles that have raged in the past hundred years over the use of water in Carson Valley. Added to the usual heated hostilities that occur among irrigators on any stream, and particularly one flowing through an oasis where the water supply is limited, were the demands of the stamp mills. There were over fifteen of these mills situated down the river from Carson City to reduce the ores from Virginia City. The principal owner of the mills was the Union Mill and Mining Company, a William Sharon enterprise, which claimed the mills' use of the waters of the Carson to be earlier than that of the ranchers of Carson Valley.

A third contender for the flow of the Carson was the logging and cord wood interests that used the stream to float their harvest cut on the slopes of the Sierra to supply the needs of the fast expanding towns of Carson and Virginia City. The many conflicts endemic in this situation came to a dramatic climax in the first days of July 1889.

The summer of 1889 was the third in succession in which drought conditions had afflicted the valley of the Carson. Everyone was "on edge." Sam Longabaugh, wood driver since 1858, was stalled with 20,000 cords of wood at McTarnahan's bridge near Carson City. The stamp mills somewhat farther down the stream were shut down. Mining and milling men were out of work. And above them in

Carson Valley, ranchers were guarding their headgates on the East Fork and its branch, the Cottonwood Slough, to see that the flow coming to them was sufficient to water their cattle and hogs and to mature their crops of grain.

The story of what happened when a dam was built across the river and all the water from the main channel was turned into the Cottonwood Slough was told some years later by the principal actors in the ensuing drama. They were then appearing as witnesses in a suit heard in the United States District Court brought by the mills and known as "The Union Mill and Mining Company vs. H.F. Dangberg et al."

Judge Daniel Webster Virgin, one of the counsels for the defense said: "State briefly what you know about the construction of that dam and turning the water in the Carson River down the Cottonwood Slough on or about the first of July, 1889."

William Dangberg answered: "The second of July I started from home for Carson. Before I left, my man came to me and told me there was not enough water in the ditches to irrigate with, and I told him to wait until the next morning and when I got back from Carson I would go up the river and see about getting more water in the ditches. I went to Carson and when I got back, I met Springmeyer (the ranch of H.H. Springmeyer got water from the Cottonwood Slough) in the sagebrush near the telegraph line, and he stopped me and said, 'William, how do you get along with the water?' and I said, 'I didn't have much water in the ditch this morning when I left.' He said, 'I heard they turned all the water in the Hogreve Slough,' and we talked a while and Mr. Fred Frevert drove up, and he asked, 'What is the news?' . . . I asked him if he could let me have some water from his ditch to irrigate my grain, and he said, 'William, when I left home I saw Carsten Henningsen and he told me they turned all the water in the Cottonwood Slough.' . . . Springmeyer looked back, and he said, 'What is that?' and Mr. Frevert told him and that made me excited, and I said, 'I will have the water down tonight, even if I don't get any in my ditch; I want the water where it belongs, or part of it, anyway.'"

General Robert M. Clarke, another counsel for the defense, asked Charles Henningsen: "Do you remember the year 1889 as to its character in point of abundance or scarcity of water?"

Charles Henningsen answered: "I do. There was not much water in 1889 at any time during the entire season. The third day of July, 1889, Mr. William Dangberg came to my place in the morning; he was very excited and said he was going up the river. He said some of the ranchers from the north side or from the Cottonwood Slough, or the millmen had turned the water down the Cottonwood Slough and the river was nearly dry. That was in the morning when he came first, and he passed on and I went on with my work, and in the afternoon at about 2 or 3 o'clock, William Dangberg and my brother came back to my place, and they said they had been over to Millerville to see Mr. Woodbury (representing the mills) and Mr. Sam Longabaugh (the wood driver) and that Sam had wood in the river and was getting stuck with it down below, and he wanted water to float his wood to Empire. They wanted

Dangberg Ranch well in operation after 1920.

81

Artesian wells in operation on the Dangberg ranches after 1920.

me to go along with them, and we agreed that if the ranchers along the Cottonwood Slough were going to turn all the water out of the river down the Cottonwood Slough, and leave us without water along the line of the river, that we would tear out their dams, and turn the water where it always run. We didn't want them to take the water out of its course and leave us without any, and we agreed that if we couldn't get any water that they should not have any either, and that the water should run where it always run, and that they could not cut us off without water (in order) to use it for themselves.

"I hitched up a team and we went to Millerville, and we wanted to see Woodbury and Longabaugh first. There we found that Longabaugh had got the water turned down the Cottonwood Slough, and I did not understand whether it was Longabaugh or the millmen that had turned the water into the Cottonwood Slough from the main river. They had turned the water into the Cottonwood Slough thinking they could get the water quicker that way and maybe more of it, and they had come back to see how it worked, and it didn't work as Longabaugh was still stuck in the river with his wood and didn't get what water he needed to float his drive. All the ditches along the line of the Cottonwood Slough were running plumb full. As soon as the ranchers found water flowing in the Slough, I suppose they let it go in their ditches, or put it in themselves."

In his further testimony, William Dangberg spelled out the dilemma of the wood drivers and the millmen: "Both Mr. Woodbury and Mr. Longabaugh said if they turned the water down the main river they would not get it where they wanted it, and they were afraid it would spread by the tules at the Hot Springs (Walley's). They kept on talking, and I said, 'I want the water down today,' and Mr. Longabaugh said, 'If you turn the water you will get into trouble.' . . . I said, 'If you can arrest me, all right; I want the water in the main river for my stock, and I want the water in the natural channel where it belongs, and if I get into trouble, I don't care.' We kept on talking that way, and they said finally, 'If you let us have the water for four days, you can after that use the water yourselves between the farmers.' . . . Woodbury said, 'If you turn it down the river, Fred Dangberg will catch it,' and I said, 'You won't miss a drop of water and he won't spread a drop on his land; I will look out that it passes his place and my place.'"

Charles Henningsen said to Longabaugh: "You have to look out for Mr. Cohn," and Longabaugh said, "That is all right; Mr. Cohn and me get along first rate . . . If you get the water down there, I will get along with the rest."

William Dangberg continued the story: "And so Carsten Henningsen and Stodieck and myself and the water man (his name was Muzzy. He was hired by and therefore represented the mills) we four went up the river, and went first and tore the dam out at what we call the Virginia ditch. . . . and we took that dam out, and that turns the water in the Hogreve Slough and the Company Ditch, and there is another ditch . . . the Upper Field Ditch, and took out Lawrence Christiansen's dam across the river, and then we went for the Cottonwood Slough, and the dam built by the water man, and we took out that dam, and then we followed down the river below the head of the Cot-

Waterfowl in Carson Valley. Writing from Carson Valley in the late 1850s, "Tennessee," correspondent of the *San Francisco Herald* said, "game such as rabbits, ducks, geese, sage-hens, antelopes, etc., is abundant and the river is crowded with fish of excellent varieties." *(From a water color, courtesy of James A. Lawrence)*

tonwood Slough, and there was another dam where we took water out called the Rocky or Middle Slough, and we took that out and let the water go down the river. From there we went to the Stodieck Ditch . . . and we took that out, and after that we went to the Lightle Ditch, and we took that dam out, and after we got that open, we went to Springmeyer's dam again and took that out, and from there Mr. Stodieck and Carsten Henningsen and Charley Henningsen went home, and then it was about 12 o'clock at night and we was all wet and tired out, and those men went home."

"I went to my brother Fred (H.F. Dangberg) and I got him out of bed, and I said, 'The water is here, and I want you to pull a couple more boards out of your dam; there is not enough water,' and he got out of bed quick, and we went to two of his dams and pulled the boards out of two of his dams, one above his house and one below. Then we followed down into Cohn's field where there is another timber dam, and that was not quite open, and we pulled that out, my brother Fred and I pulled that out." In later years William Dangberg said that it was just then that the anvils began to sound in Gardnerville to celebrate the Fourth of July.

"I went home, and the next day I went to my brother Fred and looked to see if everything was all right according to the way we agreed with Woodbury and Longabaugh, and to see if there was any water in the ditches or any spread over the land, and I didn't see a drop of water wasted; it all went down the stream according to our agreement."

Charles Henningsen took up the story: "On the Fourth of July, the day after the dams were torn out, I went to the river at my place, and I have a mark there on the rocks, and I watched that water pass my place for four days . . . every day until the last day, when it fell about three-quarters of an inch or an inch, and it was to have been the last day or the next to the last day when I should have the water on my place according to the agreement, and I couldn't get any, and I went to Fred Dangberg and told him, 'You are getting all the water,' and he said, 'No, (but) it is not reaching the wood,' and I said, 'What is the matter?' He said he didn't know; so I went with him right back to his corral, and we went to see about the water, and we saw it had not gone there. . . .

"Mr. Muzzy went through Cohn's field, and I saw him

a day or two afterwards, and he said that the water had all scattered down in Cohn's field, and that was the reason that the water didn't reach the wood."

General Clarke then asked Mr. Cohn: "Do you remember the circumstances of an agreement or understanding between the ranchers and Sam Longabaugh and J.P. Woodbury Companies (the Mills) to let them have water for four days, and they agreeing after that the ranchers should not be troubled about the water during the balance of the season?"

Mr. Cohn answered: "All there was of it was that he came to me here and asked if we would let the water go by our ranch for, I believe, four days so that he could get his wood out, and I said 'yes,' and he said 'all right, that he would go up and see the other ranchers.' I believe the conversation took place in Carson, and he went up in the evening, and I went up the next morning, and I met my foreman and I told him, 'When Sam Longabaugh wants to get his wood out, let the water go by for him, and don't touch it,' and he said, 'There is no water to touch here,' and that was all the conversation we had, and I don't think the water went to the ranch at all; Sam Longabaugh went to the ranchers, and they said, 'You go and see Cohn to see that he lets the water pass his place,' and Sam said, 'I will take care of the Jews.' "

Counsel for the prosecution, Trenmore Coffin asked Mr. Cohn: "Didn't you hear about that time, that after the four days had gone by that Longabaugh had in fact got no water?"

Mr. Cohn answered: "I heard afterwards about Sam kicking about the water, and calling some names, and I passed along there and I said, 'What is the matter, Sam?' and he said, 'They won't let the water down,' or something to that effect."

Counsel Coffin asked: "Is it not true also, that after the four days had gone by, and he had no water, that he put a force of men on the river, and then got the water down and he floated his wood down to Empire?"

Mr. Cohn replied: "I didn't hear of it, but I know he got the wood to Empire."

Counsel Coffin probed: "Can you imagine how it was that the water would run down to Empire with ten or twenty men to watch it, and it would not get down without?"

Mr. Cohn elaborated: "I don't know; we didn't hold it back. Sam said a couple years ago that the Jews always treated him well."

Counsel Coffin repeated: "You don't know why he didn't get the water to his wood drive during those four days?"

Mr. Cohn repeated: "I don't know."

Counsel Coffin became explicit: "But if I had twenty men or so standing along the banks of the river armed with clubs, would you think that had anything to do with the water flowing down so that he could float his wood to Empire?"

Mr. Cohn persisted: "I don't know."

The decree in the suit in which the foregoing testimony was taken was written by the Honorable Thomas P. Hawley and handed down on May 24, 1897. It allocated the waters of the Carson on the basis of prior appropriation. The mills had no rights earlier than 1860; rights of some of the ranchers were earlier. For those who were irrigating lands with rights later than the mills, the decree would have been disastrous had not fate intervened. The mills closed down in 1895 owing to the fact that they had no ores to process. Thus the decline of the Comstock, though it robbed the ranchers of their principal market, assured them of their precious water.

Floods on the Carson River

THE PIONEERS called it a "freshet," the great flood of December-January, 1861-1862. Describing how it came to be, years later, one of them, testifying in the suit of the Union Mill and Mining Company vs. H.F. Dangberg, said:

"There was an immense fall of snow before the flood . . . the flood was caused by warm rains following this heavy fall of snow. The ground was covered with three or four or five feet of snow . . . and it rained for three or four days and nights."

This great rush of water came at a time when the ranchers had only just established themselves on the land. Their dwellings and barns were little more than sheds; their fences made for the most part of morticed rails; their bridges, the few there were, were made of logs and timbers; their dams were made of willows and logs. Nothing could withstand the force of the water. The channel of the East Fork of the Carson changed its course; livestock were drowned. Devastation was everywhere — but not discouragement. The ranchers and the owners of toll bridges began restoration as soon as the waters subsided. Life went on in Carson Valley.

Floods, none of them as great as this one as far as it is known, have occurred in other years on the Carson River. One took place in December of 1867 and another in 1907, augmented by waters coming from the Pinenut Hills by way of the flash streams usually flowing only during cloudbursts. There have also been others: in March of 1928, December of 1937, November-December of 1950, and December of 1955. The raging, swirling waters carry uprooted trees, brush, logs from the mountains, piling up masses of debris behind dams and bridges causing the pressure of the water to wash them out or, if they hold, forcing it to spread silt-laden blankets over fields and pastures. The loads of silt dumped on the flooded areas act as fertilizer if not too deeply deposited. Too often, the rushing waters carry gravel and boulders, destroying cultivated and grass land wherever they come to rest.

In some years, the spring run-off from the melting snow in the Sierra Nevada creates near-flood conditions in the valley without the destruction of a flood. On one such occasion, a dairy farmer on the West Fork fled with his wife and his forty cows to dry land on his brother's ranch. Here the entire feminine contingent stayed from May 14 until July 10.

84

The flood of 1955, looking east from the ranch of Ted Bacon. In 1858, this was the ranch of pioneer Peter W. Van Sickle. *(Courtesy of Ted Bacon)*

The flood of 1955, looking north from the home of Ted Bacon. *(Courtesy of Ted Bacon)*

The flood of 1937, looking south from the Cradlebaugh Bridge. (*Courtesy of Juanita Schubert*)

87

ALONG THE ROAD TO ESMERALDA

The Pinenut Hills

COMING INTO Carson Valley from the south over U.S. Route 395, the motorist passes through an area where the Pinenut Range swings toward the west, narrowing the gap between its low brush and Pinyon Pine covered slopes and the lofty Sierra Nevada. These lower hills on the right were once heavily covered with the nut-bearing pine trees which supplied the principle staple in the diet of the Washoe tribe. After gathering the cones, the Indians stacked them for winter use as seen in the picture on page 90.

The coming of the white man administered a heavy jolt to this food-gathering practice. One way in which this was brought about is told in the September 5, 1863, issue of the *Virginia Daily Union* where it is noted that the great demand and high prices for wood had induced a number of Spaniards to take trains of mules into the hills to pack "immense loads of fuel into town." In this enterprise, the Spaniards were rivals of the Chinese who with diminutive donkeys no larger, the reporter says, than "a sagebrush

Hauling firewood from the Pinenut Hills. The best steam engine was purchased by the Dangberg Company in 1905. Each wagon carried five cords of wood.

Susie seated before her cache of pine cones from which she is beating the nuts.

hare,'' were engaged in delivering cord wood either to the towns or to the charcoal burners. In the Census for 1870, twenty-three Chinese were reported living in Douglas County.

The story is told of a small boy who, in the early 1880s, had been riding after cattle in these hills. As he headed home one evening, he was accosted by a very agitated Chinese, pigtail and blue cotton coattails flying, with these words in high pitched oriental tones: "Hey, boy! Hey, boy! You see my jackassee gotee jackassee shoe-blanee you sabee?''

Rivals of the Chinese, the Spaniards, and the cattlemen in exploiting the riches of the Pine Nuts were the prospectors and miners. The Jessen Brothers, coming from Schleswig-Holstein in the late 1870s, long operated the Winter's Mine, named for John B. Winters, one of the original owners. A well-paying mine was never operated until 1925 when George W. Slater filed claims to a pocket of nuggets on the western slope of Mt. Siegal. How this mine may have been discovered in 1891 is set forth by the well-known Carson City newspaperman and editor of the *History of Nevada*, Sam P. Davis, in the ballad which follows:

'Twas a dreary day at Pine Nut, and gloom was everywhere.
There was sadness in the little camp and sorrow in the air.
A more doleful set of faces one would not care to see.
The day the boys laid out the corpse of poor old Bill Magee.

'Twas pneumonia or whiskey — they couldn't quite decide
That sent the fleeting soul of Bill across the Great Divide;
But with very little wrangling over life's extinguished lamp,
They arranged a mighty funeral to advertise the camp.

I know of places where a man who shuffles off his coil
Is pitched face down with boots-on in scarce a foot of soil;
But now the boys of Pine Nut said such things had had their day,
And they'd bury Bill with socks on, in a decent Christian way.

89

Pinenut gathering — burning the pitch out of the cones.

So they hired a Carson preacher, of noted funeral skill,
And agreed on forty dollars for some extra words for Bill.
There are some parsons in the land that'd go a little higher,
But this man was no grafter, but my own illustrious sire.

At two o'clock the coffin passed through Bill's cabin door,
With Otto Schulz and Joe Raycraft and Jackson at the fore,
Tony Kramer, with his goggles, helped to hold the coffin up,
Then followed tall Miles Johnson and his little brindle pup.

Pratt, with a Heitman flour sack sewed firmly on his pants;
Bill Peckham, Baldy Adams, Lew Stevenson, Old Nance;
And loomin' up ahead of all, the big long-bearded Zern,
All headin' toward the bourn from which none can return.

They finally reached the yawning grave beneath a spreading tree,
The parson told how pure had been the life of Bill Magee;
And as they heard the kindly things the clergyman had said,
They almost thought that angel's wings was sproutin' from the dead.
They let the coffin down with hands as steady as a clock's,
And then began to shovel in the gravel on the box,
When suddenly they stopped the work. Somebody hollered "Whew!"
And then a golden nugget came a-flashin' into view.

Joe Raycraft, straddlin' o'er the grave called out, "I locate here;"
And then Lew Stevenson gave Joe a swat upon the ear;
Next Johnson jumped aboard of Lew in a most decided way,
And then the savage brindle pup plunged headlong in the fray.

Then Baldy Adams pulled his gun, and Billy Peckham his,
And in 'bout a half a second the lead began to whiz.
For several humming minutes it was a fearful fray,
With all upon the ground before the smoke had cleared away.

The parson, when he heard the shots, whipped up his old gray mare,
To find the coroner and send that functionary there.
When that official reached the spot, immediately did he
Tack a location notice on the headstone of Magee;

Remarkin' to the wounded: "I regret you can't agree.
I'll record these placer diggin's and consider it my fee."
And so before the sun was down the records were complete,
All in accordance with the law at Douglas county-seat.

And now the thrifty coroner, as many are aware,
Is livin' off that placer claim, a multi-millionaire,
While the parson oft has mentioned, confidentially to me,
From that eventful day to this he never got his fee.

Mining cabin in the Pinenut Hills about 1927. The owner from Michigan enjoying a game with the operator, Jack Quill. *(Courtesy of Evalina Quill Smith)*

Gardnerville

THE BUYING and selling of villages is not generally thought of as being a business in pioneer communities and certainly not in Carson Valley yet that is exactly what happened when Moses Job sold Sheridan to J. W. Haines in 1861. Twenty-four years later on January 13, 1885, the village of Gardnerville suffered the same fate when the owner, Lawrence Gilman, sold a half interest in it to Victor Lundergreen for the sum of $1250.

At the date of this sale, Gardnerville was six years old. This infant was the embodiment of a dream of an early-day promoter who perceived the fate that awaited Genoa in 1869 when the iron rails of the Central Pacific through Reno replaced the dust-clouded Carson River Route through Genoa.

On March 10, 1873, promoter Gilman married Mary Singleton, widow of J.T. Singleton who had owned the Nevada Hotel in Genoa. This was not a happy union. At length, spurred on by a threatened domestic disaster and the Bodie boom of 1878, Gilman purchased the Kent House, situated between Genoa and Walley's Hot Springs. He had this house, reputed to be haunted, dismantled board by board, loaded on wagons and brought to the seven-acre tract he had purchased in that same year from his friend, homesteader John M. Gardner. Here the old Kent House was re-erected and eventually became the Gardnerville Hotel. Fortunately, the ghost, who had reputedly robbed a stage on the Kingsbury Grade, did not move with the house to ply his trade in the new settlement.

Gilman made sure of a viable community by building a blacksmith shop and a saloon. Here in the center of the hay and grain-producing community on the East Fork of the Carson River was a place where the rancher could have his horses shod while he refreshed himself in the saloon and gossiped with travelers who were using the new road

The Trinity Lutheran Church. On May 26, 1895, the Trinity Evangelical Lutheran Congregation, after eighteen years of missionary work, was organized in Carson Valley. It was the first Lutheran congregation in Nevada. Henry Heitman was president, William Lampe was secretary and Henry Lange was treasurer. The church was built on land purchased from William Lampe, just south of Gardnerville on State Route 56. The first service was held on Christmas Eve, 1895, the last, in this building, on September 27, 1953. The fine new church built of brick, situated one block off Main Street in Gardnerville is the realization of the dream of the Reverend Mr. Paul H. Felten who was pastor from June 5, 1921 to June 19, 1955. *(From a water color, courtesy of James A. Lawrence)*

A Lutheran christening party in July of 1907. The third child from the right is the infant Cecil A. Stodieck seated on his mother's lap. (*Courtesy of Elvin and William Stodieck*)

Cottonwood trees at the site of the old Kent House which, in 1879, was torn down and removed to a new site to become the Gardnerville Hotel. (*From a watercolor courtesy of James A. Lawrence*)

The Gardnerville Hotel and blacksmith shop about 1880. *(Courtesy of Archie Millar)*

Gardnerville about 1895. The East Fork Hotel on the left was built by George and Charley Brown in 1893. It was improved in 1895. The Brown brothers came to Genoa in 1880 with a circus in which they performed as musicians. In Gardnerville, in 1904, they built a brickyard and formed a band. The old hotel is now the home of Mrs. Gorgonia Borda. *(Courtesy of Nevada Historical Society and Sonia DeHart)*

Gardnerville in the 1920s. On the right behind the trees is the East Fork Hotel. On the left is the Dempster Ice Cream Parlor and Hotel. *(Courtesy of Henry and Edna Frevert)*

Gardnerville before 1920. First on the right is a building brought from Virginia City about 1895 and now the J T Bar. On the far right is the Ritchford Hotel since destroyed by fire. *(Courtesy of Henry and Edna Frevert)*

The habit of moving houses to Gardnerville persisted. This is a street scene about 1915. *(Courtesy of Archie Millar)*

Papa Starke's Bar was opened in 1908 by Papa who came to Carson Valley in 1893 as a roving organ grinder later to become a cook and finally to graduate to the place behind the bar. Papa served lunches at noon; the guests were entertained by A.W.H. Helberg, who sang German songs. During World War I a group of patriots threatened hanging both proprietor and performer if this pleasant practice were continued. *(Courtesy of Mrs. Elizabeth Brown)*

Papa Starke behind his bar in the Germania Hotel. *(Courtesy of Nevada State Park Commission)*

The first store in Gardnerville about 1895. At this time the second story was the Valhalla Hall.
(Courtesy of Hans R. Jepsen and Mildred Jepsen Clark)

from this center to connect on the south with the road to Esmeralda and Bodie at the Twelve Mile House. On the northwest it connected with the Boyd Toll Road and Genoa. One suspects the hand of Lawrence Gilman behind the opening of this new road, authorized by the County Commissioners late in 1878.

The name of Gardnerville? After John M. Gardner, of course. His homestead dated from 1861. Early in its history, the village became the social center for the Danish immigrants coming to Carson Valley, after 1870, from Schleswig-Holstein. Here, L.S. Ezell, who had settled in the valley in 1864 and, like Gilman, purchased part of John M. Gardner's homestead, became, together with Carsten Henningsen, L.M. Christensen and others, the found-

ers of the Valhalla Society on January 19, 1885. Its purpose was to disseminate useful knowledge among members, particularly of our government and its laws. Its meeting place for the first twenty years was the Danish Hall which was torn down on its original site ''across the river'' and moved to a site a short distance south and east of the Gardnerville Hotel where it was rebuilt as the Valhalla Hall. On October 4, 1886, it replaced the East Fork School as the polling place of the East Fork Precinct. The East Fork School was north of the Twelve Mile House and when the Douglas County Board of Commissioners changed the polling place to the hall it became official that the center of gravity of the East Fork community had become the new village of Gardnerville.

The Methodist Church

THE OLD METHODIST church in Gardnerville was a charming, early English (Gothic) structure built in 1896 on a lot donated for this purpose by L.S. Ezell. The Reverend Mr. Theodore Taylor was then the minister of that denomination in Carson Valley. He was elected to this charge on September 9, 1892. According to one of his contemporaries, he was one of God's true and trusted men. His sermons were always based on the word of God as recorded in the Scriptures. He left the affairs of state and nation to statesmen, giving his entire time to saving souls. When the weakness of human nature knocked some indiscreet person into the gutter, it was not the saloon man who gave the unfortunate person a boost. No, indeed; it was Mr. Taylor who would pick him up, take him home and, in a few days, have him on the right track — until the next time.

Aside from holding services in Genoa, the Reverend Mr. Taylor preached in Valhalla Hall in Gardnerville before the Methodist church was built and he was the first pastor after the edifice was completed.

In 1940 it was named the Carson Valley Methodist Church by the Reverend Mr. T. Harold Grimshaw. Until recently it stood on the corner now occupied by a motel and frosty spot.

A facsimile of the first record of the Methodist Church in Carson Valley.

The Carson Valley Methodist Church. The foundation was laid in October of 1895. It was torn down in 1951 and a new edifice built north of Gardnerville. *(Courtesy of Mrs. Fred Minchin)*

How Millerville
Got on the Map

THE VILLAGE of Millerville shown on the United States Geological Survey maps of 1893 found a place on the maps of that year owing to the far-sighted generosity of the indomitable little lady who, seated in her smart buggy drawn by her spirited horse and surrounded by her husband and two children, entertained visions of immortality for her home and family.

Elizabeth Wilson, who was born in New Glasgow, Nova Scotia, came to the United States and to Genoa in 1883 where she married the Scotch blacksmith, Alexander Miller, who was at that time employed in the smithy of pioneer, Lawrence Gilman. Something of the quality of the man that charmed the young woman may be envisioned from a tale told years later by a man who, as a small boy, stood nearby in wide-eyed wonder as the sparks flew from his anvil, "What's ya makin', Miller?" To which the satisfying reply always was, "Makin' a goose's bridle!"

The home to which Miller took his young bride was brought from Virginia City. This transplanted house, Miller's blacksmith shop and the inn of Andrew Jessen, across the road, were close by the site where the survey party set up camp for their work in Carson Valley. Often at the end of a long day when the weary men who had carried their transits and compasses back to camp, started to prepare their evening meal they found, on the table in their tent, delicious hot scones, fresh-baked pies or biscuits waiting for them to lend the touch of home and titilate the famished palate. At length when the days of surveying were over the chief of party came to ask Mrs. Miller what he owed her for the delicacies. Her proud reply was, "Nothing." The chief of party then gallantly replied, "Madam, in order to commemorate your care of us while here, we will add to our maps the name *Millerville*."

The Miller house and family about 1900. *(Courtesy of Archie Millar)*

An excursion from Carson Valley to Lake Tahoe about 1896. Mrs. Miller and her two children were passengers. The driver was Dick Henderson whose regular work was hauling charcoal from the Pinenut Hills. *(Courtesy of Archie Millar)*

The Ferris House

T HE GHOSTLY old house standing, until 1942, in a field a mile to the north of Minden and west of U.S. Highway 395 had several times in the one hundred odd years of its life been concerned with happenings that received national notice. Built in 1865 with nails hammered out on the anvils of Henry Van Sickle, plastered with lime reinforced with horse hair, it was graced with a marble-faced fireplace in the parlor. For five years it was the home of G.W.G. Ferris, his wife and his family of four girls and three boys. This family came by wagon and carriage direct from Galesburg, Illinois, in three months of travel. They immediately earned the sobriquet of "the emigrants." This name was also given to the ditches G.W.G. Ferris built.

The Ferris family was probably the only family of such size living away from the Carson River Route. With two teen-age sons to help with the farming and with a marriageable daughter, they made a decided impression among the neighboring bachelors and the few couples who occupied the nearby homesteads. On March 15, 1866, the oldest daughter, Maggie, became the wife of H.F. Dangberg to whom she had been introduced by her cousin Chauncy N. Noteware, Nevada's first Secretary of State. This had occurred at a dinner Mr. and Mrs. Noteware held on the September evening of the Ferris family's arrival in Carson City.

The Ferris family had sold their dairy and cheese plant in Illinois for $60,000. On arrival in western Nevada, in 1864, and due to the exigencies of the Civil War, their money was worth but fifty cents on the dollar which prohibited their going, as originally intended, to settle in San Jose, California, where the older children had planned to go to school.

The youngest member of the family, Mame, suffering from rheumatic fever, was brought across the plains on a pillow. She was restored to health on the long trek. Mame lived to be 98 years old and to record in her later years a child's recollections of the life of "the emigrants" in Carson Valley. Night after night while she waited in the dusk for her father to finish the milking and join her for her daily lesson in astronomy, the little girl was awed by the great silence that engulfed all below the brilliant firmament. This frontier world was so silent, so vastly lonely.

The second youngest member of the emigrant family was George Washington Gale who became the distinguished bridge builder of the 1890s and the inventor of the Ferris wheel, the sensational attraction of the World's Fair in Chicago in 1893. The spark of inspiration for the wheel

The Ferris house. *(Courtesy of Juanita Schubert)*

George Washington Gale Ferris, born February 14, 1859, near Galesburg, Illinois; died November 22, 1896.

came to the lad as he watched the flutter wheel at Cradlebaugh's bridge over the Carson River, situated about six miles north of the boy's home. Sister Maggie's husband provided the tuition which took the young inventor from Carson Valley to Oakland and then finally to Rensselaer Polytechnic School in Troy, New York. From Rensselaer Ferris went on to his fame.

About 1870 the Ferris family left their ranch in Carson Valley in fear of an Indian attack which never occurred. One of the teen-age sons, late in the evening, had caught a native thief in the watermelon patch. With ill-considered haste and judgment, he ran for his shotgun and shot into the ground just behind the Washoe, or so he thought. Not so! The shot nicked the thief's heel. The tribesmen vowed revenge. The family, fearful of a massacre, moved to Carson City.

After the flight of the Ferris family their ranch was purchased by H.F. Dangberg. It was thereafter leased to families who attended to the irrigating of the surrounding pastures. About 1883 a family by the name of Sarman was so employed and, while they were tenants, the second event to attract the attention of the outside world occurred. There were three members of the family: the mother, the father and a son, William. The old people in their sixties were German immigrants who spoke little English.

On the morning of May 8, 1895, Mr. Sarman remained around the house later than usual to see his good wife set out food for a tramp. Mrs. Sarman had more than her fair share of unwelcome visitors. Tramps often passed her house, which stood at the joining of the Boyd road from Genoa and the Cradlebaugh road from Carson. She feared that one of the drifters would one day murder her. After lunch on this day in May, with his shovel over his shoulder, Mr. Sarman left the house to walk the miles of ditches, spreading water over the pastures.

About four o'clock Mr. Sarman returned to see smoke curling from the doors and windows of the house. Calling to his wife he hurried forward, grabbed a bucket and began throwing water into the smoke-filled parlour and into the bedroom where the fire was burning. After throwing bucket upon bucket of water on the burning bedstead the smoke subsided. At this moment a man on foot passed by on his way from Bridgeport, California, to Genoa. Mr. Sarman called him in. The stranger could see that a charred body lay on the bed, but could not understand German, hence, could not get any further information from the frantic old man. He continued on the road to Boyd's to spread the alarm.

When the sheriff and coroner arrived at the scene they discovered blood stains on the parlor floor where murder had been done. Later the blood-covered hatchet was found in the woodshed. The crime had been committed as often envisioned by Mrs. Sarman. The criminal? The man who had the eleven o'clock lunch at the kind hands of the aging woman was found and brought to Genoa for questioning only to be released on his own recognizance. At one time when the sheriff seemed hesitant, lynching was threatened.

The newspapermen of the valley had a field day, proposing to solve all the evils of society by "doing something" about tramps. Nothing was ever done, however, despite the exercises in hyperbole. From time to time in the succeeding years, tramps in the western states have turned in confessions telling how the crime was committed. The mystery remains unsolved to this day.

Dreams, horror, and miracles belong to the old house. Dreams of a young lad translated into an invention acclaimed at a world's fair, a murder previsioned by the victim and widely reported in the press of the day, and, finally, a multiple birth are all part of this house. Eight years after the murder, an accomplished and lovely young woman, twenty-year-old Viola who had come from Walla Walla, Washington as the bride of Henry Berning, lived here. On October 17, 1903, she gave birth to triplet girls; two lived, the third died. The young mother lived only a little longer than this third child then her life slowly ebbed away. This was the first and last birth of triplets in Carson Valley.

Mrs. Edith Merrick, wife of the manager of the Douglas County Creamery, was sure that such an event deserved recognition in the national capital. Information had it that President Theodore Roosevelt had offered a one thousand dollar bonus to the parents of triplets. The president's secretary, in a letter dated on the day of Mrs. Berning's death, extended congratulations to the young parents, but did not enclose a check.

Cradlebaugh Bridge

THE CRADLEBAUGH Bridge, the first across the Carson River in Carson Valley, was not, as one might suppose, named for Judge John Cradlebaugh who was appointed a judge of the United States District Court and assigned to Carson County, Utah Territory, in 1859. Instead, it was named for the judge's younger brother, William.

Young William found life somewhat tedious in the east. He was a lively fellow, therefore the family decided that he should be encouraged to go west where opportunity for the use of excess energy and budding talent was reported to be excellent. The young man started out to find his brother. Several years later, on foot and famished, he arrived on the Carson River where Uncle Tommy Bowers, uncle of the well-known stagecoach driver Jim Kane, was operating the Pony Saloon. William had exactly fifty cents in his pocket. He inquired the price of a dinner and was told that a dinner cost one dollar. Undaunted, William said,

"Then give me half a dinner," and laid down his fifty cents. Uncle Tommy, being a kindly and understanding man, gave the starved young wanderer a whole dinner and set him on the way to his brother, the judge, in Genoa.

It was a good five miles to Genoa where several hours later William arrived — again starving. Here he appropriately ate turnip peelings. This vegetable was being prepared at the watering trough for an upcoming dinner at one of the hotels. The outer covering of this luxury item, which Colonel John Reese had sold for a dollar a bunch in 1852, held body and soul together until the Judge arrived a few hours later.

Two years after his near-starvation, young William, under the guidance of his brother, set himself up as a toll road operator and built, in 1861, the bridge which thereafter bore his name. The toll road, known as the Cradlebaugh Road, shortened the distance from Carson City to the mines of Esmeralda by eight miles. In 1860, James Morgan operated a saddle train over this road which carried passengers from Carson City to Aurora.

Early in 1862, the bridge was washed out in the great storm of that year, usually called the "freshet." William Cradlebaugh answered the challenge of the elements and immediately rebuilt the bridge. In possession of this useful

Wood drive halted at a bridge across the Carson typical of a number of bridges in Carson Valley. This picture was taken on one of the last drives to Empire. *(Courtesy of Nevada State Museum)*

Uncle Tommy Bowers about 1903 when he lived at Mc-Tarnahan Bridge. In the 1860s he was proprietor of the Pony Saloon and is said at one time to have delivered a baby. *(Courtesy of Nevada State Park Commission)*

crossing for the rest of his life, William became venerable — the Uncle Billy of many a tale. Some years after the building of the bridge, he was joined by his sister Leoline and her husband, Ira Lewis. The sprightly young matron was importuned, a few years later, to become a school teacher. "But how?" she asked the visiting superintendent, "How should I teach school when I can't even spell?"

Undaunted on his "talent" hunt, the superintendent opened his book and began quizzing the young mother. She did very well. Then he pronounced the word "seize." Leoline spelled it correctly. However, when he sprang upon her the word "siege," she hesitated for an instant until the trustee who accompanied the visiting superintendent winked conveniently, whereupon she came off with flying colors by placing the "i" before the "e." And so the Jack's Valley School acquired a teacher for that year.

Living or visiting at the bridge was a delight to young fry in the Cradlebaugh and Lewis families. Here all the excitement of a tie-up in the wood drive would bring hordes of drivers to the station. Often a curious young lad came to view the flutter wheel with which Uncle Billy kept the horse watering troughs filled to capacity with the sparkling waters of the Carson. Occasionally a rancher would leave his lunch for the children while he rode down the river with Uncle Billy. In the lunch basket could be found all sorts of unusual dainties; for instance, a glass of freshly picked strawberries from one of the upstream gardens!

The Desert Road and Station

IN 1884, D. E. WILLIAMS became editor and owner of the *Genoa Courier,* on which he had served as an apprentice printer. Mr. Williams, recalling the happenings of those years, says:

"There were many thrilling events to be recorded by a paper in those early days. The Bodie boom was on and brought much prosperity to Carson Valley farmers because the heavy freight business from Carson City through the Valley brought a big demand for hay and barley.

"The teams came up from Carson by way of the old Cradlebaugh bridge, past the Desert Station, the Twelve Mile House at the upper end of the Valley where the East Fork emerges from the mountains, and on out by way of Rodenbaugh's Station, Carter's, Holbrook's, and on through Antelope Valley and Bridgeport (presently Route 395) to the booming camp of Bodie.

"As the ten to sixteen horse teams plodded their weary way across the desert from Cradlebaugh's to the Desert Station east of Genoa we could look across the Valley and see the great clouds of dust rising, indicating the number of teams on that part of the road. But there was a difference in the clouds of dust, for there were the Fast Freight teams of Keyser & Elrod which included twenty-four horses to each string of wagons and those horses went at a pretty lively walk. One could easily pick out the fast freight teams by the rapidly rising clouds of dust. The teams traveled day and night and lost but a few minutes in changing horses at the stations. When they pulled in at Desert Station, for instance, there would be a string of 24 fresh horses all hooked up to their stretchers and lead chains. When the team stopped, the driver dismounted and men turned in and unhitched the wheelers, dropped the lead chain from the point of the tongue and the string of horses moved away and the string of fresh horses pulled right in. The lead chain was hooked up, the wheeler's tugs hooked, the driver mounted his near wheeler, pulled up the jerk line and quicker than one can tell the story these big fast freight wagons were moving at a lively pace."

Others recall that on still nights the twinkling of lanterns on the lead horses could be seen and the tinkling of the bells on their bridles could be heard even in Genoa! The use of the road declined when the boom in Bodie faded.

Other not-so-well-documented tales of the road have to do with it after it left the desert and passed into the hills farther south. On the hill east of Holbrook's, now called The Mountain House, stood a fort where the freight lines hauling the bullion from Bodie to the mint in Carson City kept two riflemen to guard the loaded wagons as they passed through the gap below. A stage robbery was once "pulled off" at this point and the loot buried to the west of U.S.

The Desert Station. It was removed from its original site on the road to Esmeralda to the Buckeye Ranch of the Dangberg Company in 1905. *(Courtesy of Sheila Smith Sepulveda)*

Highway 395. It has long been thought that some Indians dug it up inasmuch as after the robbery they lived extremely well without ever working.

Many are the tales told of the ghost towns of the west but what of the ghost stations and the ghost roads? Here in Carson Valley we have both. The stations are haunted not only by teamsters and miners but by those who danced to the strains of a harmonica or the strings of a fiddle as did those guests who gathered, on September 12 of 1879, at the Desert Station to enjoy a "ship hop" as it was advertised, and again a dance on June 18, 1880.

Those who drove out across the desert after the Desert Road and Station were abandoned recall the blacksmith shop as a heap of decaying boards, the two wells filled with sand, the old station with windows broken or pilfered, sand and trash blown high around it, while inside the nests of pack rats and other vermin exuded a musty odor that even the desert winds could not allay.

Occasional uses for the abandoned building were found such as that made of it in a hotly contested election in the first years of this century. All votes were eagerly sought by the supporters of each candidate for the state senate. Five of the voters were woodchoppers in the Pinenut Hills who were in the bag for the candidacy of their employer,

or so he thought.

The confident candidate brought them into Gardnerville election eve, putting them to sleep in the cloak room of Valhalla Hall. Later in the night, the opposition, learning of their hide-out, began its "dirty work." These men got the woodchoppers woefully drunk, loaded them into the back of a buckboard and drove them out to accommodations in the Desert Station where, on a rickety old table, they placed bottles of whiskey, cheese and crackers — in this instance not for rats — and left them. The woodchoppers revived late on election day and for some time did not know where they were, nor did their employer. At long last they recovered sufficiently to walk into town *after* the polls were closed. Their employer lost the election by ten votes!

The "Desert Road" was subsequently put to constructive use in quite a different manner albeit over strenuous opposition. Briefly stated, the busy old road after the decline of Bodie, was demoted to the status of a ditch. This was the *work* of H.F. Dangberg who, in spite of being enjoined by the court as early as 1865 to refrain from running water on sage brush land, persisted in this wanton practice throughout the remaining years of the century. The Desert Road was handy for this purpose. In this

107

A land clearing and ditch digging crew — scrapers on wagon, cook house, feed rack on wagon, horses and mules — ready to leave ranch headquarters for several weeks' work bringing sagebrush land under cultivation. Before 1905.

he was encouraged not only by the great demand for hay and barley — thus extended acreage for growing crops — but also by the observation that running silt-bearing flood waters over desert land built soil. He was a builder and took pleasure in cooperating with nature. The land he built from the water carried by the "Desert Road" is now known as the Haybourn Tract.

Dangberg was opposed in this practice by T.B. Rickey, a rival cattleman living in Antelope Valley, Mono County, California, who drove his herds to the rail head in Carson City over the Desert Road, if it was passable. Thus Rickey was reversing a practice that began, in 1858, when great numbers of cattle were driven in the opposite direction to the thriving market afforded by the mines of Esmeralda. Complaints of the abuse of the road were heard throughout the 1890s. The Douglas County Commissioners issued orders to Dangberg to build a new road which he agreed to do in 1903. However, fate intervened: Dangberg died in 1904. In the following year, the Virginia and Truckee Railway was extended into Carson Valley, obviating any necessity for such a road.

A Death in the Desert

IT WAS A LAZY summer's afternoon. We were sitting quietly on the porch behind the screen sipping lemonade. Beyond the garden, myriad spider webs fastened to the tops of the alfalfa plants caught the rays of the lowering sun in shimmering brilliance. Suddenly behind me at the end of the porch a tense voice said "de-su!" "Now what?" thought I, as I turned to see the distraught face of the speaker. Something was obviously very wrong on this lovely afternoon. Susie's salutation "my frind" was a plea for help. I went to the door, she came toward me, "de-la" the Washoe words for "my mother"

were spoken in still more, to me, distressful accents.

"Yes, what is it, Susie?" I said.

"My muddah, she no talk to me, she no look to me." Susie's eyes, small black beads by now, had a wild, untamed terror about them as she went on, "You gettum automobile, takkum me town pfinnum my brudder, Pete!"

"Yes, yes," I said as I ran out the door to the car, Susie followed me and climbed into the back seat. I started the engine, reached back to close the car door and we were off for town. In Gardnerville back of the blacksmith shop of pioneer Mason Krummes where the Washoes were absorbed in a great gambling game, we found Pete. Susie rushed over to the gamblers sitting in the shade of an old cottonwood, surrounded by rusting scrap iron and broken pieces of wagon wood. A word was spoken to Pete and he followed her back to the car and in a moment we were off for the wiki-up where the old woman was dying. My passengers were tense and silent — my own eyes dimmed by a tear.

In moments we had driven the two miles to the bank of the river where Susie and her mother lived. My passengers alighted and went toward the cabin and in the door. I sat absorbed in thoughts on death, especially death as it was happening to these Stone Age friends of mine; the bent little old woman with her toothless smile and her limp would no longer trudge the dusty roads burdened by her loaded cornucopia basket carried by a strap over her head.

At long last the door of the cabin opened and Susie came out to the car. I started to speak a word of sympathy. She spoke first, "He aw light, Pete he wakkum up, my muddah no die, he sleep dat's all."

"Oh, Susie," said I, looking down at her unlaced shoes, her soot-soiled dress, "too bad you scare, you run so far!"

"Ye-es!" said Susie, "me oppul scare, me likke ketchum Pete, nen dat old woman die my house, I gotta burnum ebberyting, my close, my dishes, my sewing machine, ebberyting!"

Susie and her mother beside their native "house" built of bands of twisted willow and rushes covered with sacking. They hold their seed beaters, gathering baskets and winnowing baskets. The conical basket slung by a band from the mother's head is a carrying basket. These comprise stone age woman's kitchen utensils. *(Courtesy of John Mereen)*

NEW WAYS OF LIFE

Dairies and Creameries

THE DAIRY industry of Carson Valley had its beginning in the first years of the Carson River Route. Captain J. H. Simpson, surveying for a shorter road between Salt Lake and Genoa in 1859, observed that the butter of Carson Valley was "of a rich gold color" and commanded a higher price in the Sacramento Valley than California butter.

The ranchers of Carson Valley continued to make butter for the next quarter of a century, improving neither their techniques nor their dairy stock. In 1879, and the years following, according to Owen Jones, improvements were made in the dairy stock in response to the example of J.W. Marsh, who with his sons Wilbur and William came to live on the one hundred and sixty acre ranch on the southeast corner of the Dressler Lane where it leads on to State Route 88. The property had been purchased earlier in 1879 by his wife, a popular school teacher and accomplished equestrienne. Marsh and his sons brought pedigreed, registered, short-horned Durham dairy cattle into the valley.

The original foundation stock of a great many of the present dairy herds came from the Marsh herd of Durham short-horns. Before the Marshes came with their herd, the cows of the valley, with one or two exceptions, were very ordinary. The early day farmer always thought "that a cow was a cow" and that was all there was to it. After the other farmers saw what the Marshes were doing with their herd, they changed their attitudes and began to think of improving not only their breeding but also of changing their methods of handling dairy stock.

The Marshes sold out in 1887. Their ranch, after belonging to the Dressler family, was purchased by Dietrich Thran who, in 1914, built the fine house now standing at the crossroads.

Following the decline of the mining activity that had afforded the farmers of Carson Valley a ready market not only for homemade butter but more importantly for their hay and grain for over twenty-five years before 1884, there arose a very urgent need for a cash crop to replace the defunct one of feed for teams and livestock. Dell Williams who became publisher and editor of the *Genoa Courier* on September 12, 1884, continues the story in the *Record Courier* (of September 10, 1957, Gardnerville):

"The farmers were in a quandary to know what to do. This was in the early 1890s. One day an East Fork farmer came to the *Courier* office and told me that a man working for him received a home paper from back in Wisconsin that told a great deal about what the farmers back there were doing by going into the creamery business. I asked him to bring the paper in and he did a few days later. I wrote an article about the subject and in a week or so we called a meeting of farmers at Gardnerville on Sunday. There was a good response and the movement to organize a creamery company started. It developed rapidly."

Though Mr. Williams does not say so, this organization was probably the Carson Valley Creamery which was founded on May 13, 1891. The trustees were John Frantzen, C.M. Henningsen, C.C. Henningsen, Fred Hellwinkel, Chris Larson, Wilhelm (William) Dangberg, H.F. Dangberg, Peter Heitman, William Lampe and others.

Mr. Williams recalls that a creamery man who was a "slick organizer" came in and put the creamery business on its feet. From what ensued, it appears that the "slick organizer," a Julius Kaupisch, more or less took over the operation of the Carson Valley Creamery. He and his brother Frantz formed a partnership called Kaupisch Brothers. The partnership acquired land from H.F. Dangberg on the northwest corner of the intersection of State Route 88 and the Mottsville Lane for their building. This was on August 20, 1891. On November 10 of the same year, they deeded the property to the Nevada Creamery and Commercial Company of which Evan Williams of Empire was the president. On October 7, 1892 this company deeded the land and the creamery building to the California-Nevada Creamery Company of which Williams was also president. The Surveyor General of Nevada in his *Biennial Report* for 1889-1890, noted that there were three creameries in Carson Valley but does not name them. They could have been this one, the Springmeyer Creamery and one in Fredericksburg, or that of Harrison Berry in

110

Fairview who, in 1881, milked 100 cows.

Evan Williams, the president of the California-Nevada Company was also superintendent of the Union Mill and Mining Company, a Sharon Estate subsidiary. The California-Nevada Creamery and other property was mortgaged on January 3, 1893, to the Bullion and Exchange Bank of Carson City for the sum of $50,000. According to Clarence Henningsen, son of C.M. Henningsen, the creamery company was at this time operating three creameries: one in Smith's Valley, one in Fredericksburg, and the one in Carson Valley. This enterprise was being promoted by the Reno Board of Trade, an organization formed by Francis G. Newlands as trustee for the Sharon Estate. It was part of an elaborate plan for the development of western Nevada — a plan which, if successful, would salvage, so the promoters thought, some of the assets of the estate which were rapidly depreciating in value following exhaustion of the ores on the Comstock.

The Board of Trade, through its secretary Robert L. Fulton, also land agent for the Central Pacific Railroad, received word in January of 1892 that the farmers of Carson

Valley were "very much dissatisfied" with Kaupisch. It seems that Kaupisch was paying for the milk delivered to the creamery on the basis of its butterfat content which was easily altered by the addition of a little water to the test tubes!

It then became apparent that the "slick" Mr. Kaupisch had two strikes against him: one, he was tied to activities of the Sharon Estate, through Evan Williams of Empire. Mr. Williams was superintendent of The Union Mill and Mining Company, the "deadly enemy" of Carson Valley which was at that time trying to take the irrigation water away from the farmers in a suit pending in the U.S. District Court. Two, he was accused of the little aqueous maneuver in the test tubes. Added to these strikes was a third which unmistakably branded the man, in the eyes of the local dairymen, as an unregenerate rascal; namely, his unmerciful beating of his thirteen-year-old stepson for hanging his bridle and saddle on the wrong hooks in the barn!

Mr. Williams concludes his tale with the remark that "the farmers dropped Kaupisch like a hot potato." They went across the road and put up their own creamery on land of C.M. Henningsen. This was the Douglas County

The Douglas County Creamery about 1900. The long ramp on which the team and wagon stand was designed by the first manager, C.E. Merrick, to employ to the greatest extent possible the principle of gravity in operating the creamery. The hauling of milk to the creamery and of butter to market, that is, to the railhead in Carson City provided work for teams and revenue for ranchers.
(Courtesy of Anna Neddenriep Dressler)

The Holstein dairy herd on the William Stodieck ranch about 1940. *(Courtesy of James A. Lawrence)*

Creamery Company, incorporated on May 24, 1893, for the purpose of manufacturing butter, cheese, and condensed milk, as well as to raise, grow and fatten hogs and other animals and manufacture hams and bacons. The trustees were John Frantzen, C.M. Henningsen, H.C. Dangberg, Fritz Heise, and Christ Rabe. Among those subscribing to the original issue of stock were A.F. Dressler, William Dangberg, William Lampe, William Settelmeier, and others. This creamery was a success from the start.

The California-Nevada Creamery, in spite of the appearance of a rival and the defection of a number of its patrons, apparently continued to operate until November 12, 1896, when the building was deeded to William Dangberg of the Douglas Packing Company. This organization, founded in 1892, used its cold storage facilities. The operation of this small company was a very necessary concomitant to the profitable operation of a creamery for the reason that some use had to be found for the great quantities of milk from which the cream for making butter was extracted. This milk was stored in great vats which emptied by gravity on piles of barley. It thus provided an excellent mash for the fattening of hogs. The operation was in the care of Victor Lundergreen, occupant of the little house still standing south of the creamery. For many years, the company sold several wagon loads of hogs a month, hauled live by Heise and Lampe, to the rail head in Carson City.

Soon after it went into operation, the founders of the Douglas County Creamery sent a committee of farmers to San Francisco where they secured a contract to supply the Palace Hotel and other high class establishments with their excellent butter — butter which was awarded the gold medal at the Mid-Winter Fair in San Francisco in 1894. In consequence of the founding of the new creamery, the dairymen began to build new dairy barns; among the first of these was the one on the William Settelmeier ranch.

The activity in the early 1890s in founding, building and operating creameries in Carson Valley had a very marked effect on the statistics of butter production in Douglas County.

In 1892, the Surveyor General noted in his *Biennial Report* that butter production in that year was 231,000 pounds. This was an increase from around 20,000 pounds per year as shown in several previous reports. This record was achieved by the three creameries and may or may not have included that produced by Mrs. Hugh Hansen who delivered her delicious homemade butter to Walley's Hot

Before the advent of the milking machine. *(Courtesy of Fred H. and Irma Settelmeyer)*

The Douglas County Creamery closed down in 1914 for lack of milk to process, its patrons having gone to the Minden Butter Manufacturing Company situated at the railhead in Minden. During the twenty-one years that the Douglas County Creamery was in operation, Fritz Heise, one of the founders, served faithfully and competently as treasurer, and C.M. Henningsen and later Louis Stodieck served as secretaries. These men lived within walking distance of one another; it was a familiar old world sight at the end of each month to see one or the other walking across the fields to the home of his neighbor to reconcile accounts.

The Minden Butter Manufacturing Company was founded on March 7, 1908, by R.W. and Dick Bassman, Fritz Schacht, H. Luhrs, Dick Fricke, William Dangberg, and C.E. Merrick. Stock was issued to the named founders and to the H.F. Dangberg Land and Live Stock Company and to W.F. Dressler. This company's butter, sold under the Windmill Brand, perpetuated the reputation of Carson Valley butter on the San Francisco market.

The company was reorganized as a cooperative in 1946. At length, burdened with obsolete equipment and inadequate planning for financing its replacement, this company too endured the agonies of slow death only to be replaced in 1959 by the James Canyon complex, north of Genoa. This impressive establishment is presently owned and operated by the nationally known Beatrice Foods. At long last, the independent farmers of Carson Valley have lost control of the market outlet for their milk.

Springs Resort, and the equally fine butter made by Nevada's first woman settler, Mrs. A.M. Taylor (formerly Mrs. Israel Mott), who delivered her butter to the Glenbrook Inn at Lake Tahoe. It is true, as A.F. Dressler, one of the largest dairymen in the valley, recalled some years later that dairying and the making of butter was a fine business. Witness to this fact was the building of fine homes, "butter-built" homes we may say, on the dairy ranches in Carson Valley in the early 1900's such as those of Dressler and C.M. Henningsen, still lived in by their descendants.

Milking time in a model A barn — the beginning of the process that delivers bacteria-free milk to babies. *(Courtesy of Marvin and Evelyn Settelmeyer)*

113

Waterloo

THE ACTIVITY in creamery promotion and operation that centered at the crossing of the Mottsville Lane and State Route 88 provided the impetus that led to the building of the hamlet of Waterloo in the middle 1890s. Almost immediately there arises the question, "Why Waterloo?" Indeed, *why* did the German-born Heinrich Behrmann give the name of the renowned battle to a lusterless settlement in the New World?

Inquiry has proven fruitless. To be sure, two battles in Carson Valley focused on Waterloo; namely, that of the dairymen against Kaupisch, the "slick" operator of the California-Nevada Creamery who was reducing the butterfat content of the milk with *aqua pura*, and the other, an ecclesiastical affair between two factions of the Lutheran church in which one wanted the new church to rise in Waterloo, the other in or near Gardnerville. The Gardnerville faction won this battle.

Neither of these word-waged battles seems to justify naming the settlement Waterloo. While they were going on, however, the romantic and heroic atmosphere suggested by the name may be seen to have been sustained by the arrival of Adolph Rolfs, a conqueror of sorts. On the boat that brought him to our shores, he so impressed himself upon a fellow passenger, a certain young lady whose destination was her family's home in Chicago, that she opted instead for Adolph and Waterloo. On December 23, 1895, Adolph bought the eight acres situated at the crossroads and also the blacksmith shop with tools, old iron and some timber. He subsequently built himself a house here. After their romance ended, the Rolfs' house was bought by Henry Neddenriep of Diamond Valley in 1907.

At this time, other changes were taking place in Water-

The Waterloo Resort. *(Courtesy of Anna Heise)*

loo. The old California-Nevada Creamery building was occupied as a store downstairs and a dwelling upstairs by the Goldstein family. Daughter Becky gave music lessons to the farmers' daughters, her sister Annie sewed for the farmers' wives, and son Louie became, in time, the first principal of the Gardnerville High School.

The greatest change, however, was wrought by H.W.F. Luhrs who purchased the Behrmann property, the bar and boarding house where German farm hands could live on reasonable terms during the slack winter months. After the purchase on July 8, 1907, Luhrs proceeded to build an open-air dance pavilion where, for a number of years thereafter, the German community of Carson Valley celebrated a transplanted Schutzenfest and Erntefest with kings and queens of mirth and gaiety chosen each year. The king was the winning marksman and he chose his queen.

Thus at long last fate may have decreed that there should be a belated reason for calling the hamlet Waterloo. Here Lord Byron could have heard on more than one occasion, as he did before the great battle of Waterloo on June 18, 1815, "a sound of revelry by night."

Minden and the Virginia and Truckee Railway

A RAILROAD IN Carson Valley was first openly talked of in 1876. A survey was made of a line to run from Carson City to Genoa; it came to nought. Before this, however, in the bitterly contested gubernatorial election of 1870, it was rumored in Carson Valley that the Republican candidate, F. A. Tritle, if elected, would levy on the taxpayers of Douglas County the same sort of contribution toward the building of a railroad that had been successful in raising funds to build the Virginia and Truckee in Storey and Washoe counties. Tritle was one of the incorporators of the V&T and was supposed to be a favorite of the feared and hated Bank of California.

The V & T freight depot in Minden before the passenger depot was added. The agent lived in a converted box car on a siding. About 1908. *(Courtesy of Walter S. Young)*

The Virginia and Truckee Engine Number 27 on its run to Minden, January 1, 1942. *(Courtesy of Juanita Schubert)*

Stock watering troughs alongside the V & T tracks at the shipping point a mile north of Minden.

Minden about 1915. On the left is the C.O.D. Garage. In the center is the Farmers Cooperative Mercantile Co. On the right is the V & T freight station. *(Courtesy of Ronald Custis)*

117

The first store in Minden was a branch of Meyers Mercantile of Carson City. It was opened in 1907. *(Courtesy of William Nelson)*

The V & T local headed by Engine No. 12 swinging around the "Y" into Minden about 1910. *(Courtesy of Walter S. Young)*

A ten-mule team pausing in front of the Minden livery stable. The wagons are loaded with sacks of grain for delivery to Tonopah and Goldfield, about 1909.

Sounding taps on the day of the last run, led by Pierre Ithurburu on the left. *(Courtesy of Bruce and Janet Johnson)*

John S. Child, merchant and stock raiser, living in Genoa since 1854 and also a candidate for the state assembly as a Republican, changed his party for this campaign to the "People's" party (later he switched to the Democratic Party) to defeat the feared Tritle and his supposedly nefarious intentions. During the campaign, the ladies derived no little amusement from the issues: Mrs. Child, according to her niece, Arlie Jennison, plagued her husband by attributing a sore throat to her vocal exertions at a Republican rally where she vowed she had shouted herself hoarse for Tritle!

In 1879, it was proposed to extend the Virginia and Truckee Railroad (it was called Railway after reorganization in 1905) through Douglas County to Bodie. In 1892, pressure was brought on the people of Carson Valley to float bonds for the construction of a railroad. Nine years later in 1901, the extension of the Virginia and Truckee to Carson Valley was again under consideration. Nothing more was done until, in 1905, it was proposed to extend the railroad into Alpine County.

Finally, in April of 1906, the laying of a track was begun from Carson City over a right of way donated by the H.F. Dangberg Land and Live Stock Company. The road was completed and the first passenger train ran into the newly founded town of Minden on the morning of August 1, 1906.

Prior to the building of the line the selection of a site for terminal facilities became the subject of a prolonged and bitter controversy. A site in Gardnerville was considered. It soon became evident that the extent and cost of the land would be prohibitive whereupon the Dangberg Company offered to donate land. The offer was accepted by the V&T. On the day that the first train ran into Minden the Dangberg Company and the railroad signed articles of agreement providing for construction and maintenance by the latter of livestock shipping facilities at a point one mile north of Minden.

Concurrently land and lots free of charge were offered by the Dangberg Company to the principal businessmen in Gardnerville to induce them to remove their establishments to the vicinity of the railhead in Minden. Patriotism prevailed. These offers were rejected.

The principal promoter of the town and the related development was H.F. Dangberg, Jr., son of the founder of the Company, and its secretary. It was in the village of Halle near the Prussian town of Minden, Westphalia, that H.F. Dangberg, Sr., who settled in Carson Valley in 1856, was born; hence the name Minden.

The Virginia and Truckee Railway Company extended its line into Carson Valley to provide shipment by rail for the livestock operators in the Valley and points south. The long trains of cattle cars moving cattle and sheep into Carson Valley to feed on its pasture and hayfields and of fattened cattle and sheep moving out to markets in San Francisco and even to distant Chicago were familiar sights to all Valley residents from 1906 until 1925 when similar shipments began to be made by truck.

Owing in part to the business afforded the Virginia and Truckee by Carson Valley, the historic old railroad was kept operating in the black until about 1924. It continued for a quarter of a century after this to run a freight and passenger service. The last train to run over the track came into Minden on May 31, 1950, it left for the last time on the same day.

Cattle

TENNESSEE, THE unidentified correspondent of the *San Francisco Herald*, residing in Genoa between 1857 and 1860, gave evidence of a flair for defining the inherent characteristics of areas when he named Carson Valley "the paradise of quadrapeds." Thousands of quadrapeds, even scavenger dogs, enjoyed life in Carson Valley. The assessor, in 1874, found 1,000 canines doing their bit for mankind. However, so unappreciative was he of their function that he valued man's best friend at only ½ cent per head! Quadrapeds were everywhere; not, however, the sleek white-faced Hereford and black Angus the motorist sees to-day grazing in the roadside pastures or holding up traffic on interstate highways.

One may gain some notion of the gap that separates cattle of today from those of the middle of the last century by comparing them with the motley mongrels that were divided between Dangberg and Mast when they dissolved partnership December 12, 1860. Cattle such as these represented the dairy stock of emigrants and the breeds and crossbreeds of every description that were brought together by business men when going up and down the Mississippi Valley looking for bargains. Ira M. Luther, as early as 1853, found that the drain of the westward migration of man and beast had already pushed the price per head of cows to $18 and $25, straining the financial resources of him who would drive a herd to the far west. In this same year, Ben Palmer drove 500 head from the Missouri to Carson Valley. The value of cattle once they reached Carson Valley may be illustrated by the record of a wagon sale by an emigrant in 1859. This man refused coin in payment, giving as his reason, in Pike County English, that he wanted something with "huffs" to it. "Dem ar things," he said, referring to the coins, "don't have carves."

Thousands of cattle perished in the 1850s on the long trek down the Humboldt River. Those that reached the lower Carson River with bones still held together by their hides and able to walk were often sold for panned gold to young men, such as Dangberg and Mast. These enterprising pioneers drove them to Carson Valley where they were put to feed on grass growing in the alluvium pockets along the banks of the Carson — grass that grew as high as a man's head or, if the man was mounted, it could be knotted in front of the pommel of his saddle. Small wonder then that William H. Boyd, builder of the Boyd Toll Road in 1861, who had driven a herd of cattle to California in 1858, returned with this herd to Carson Valley in August of 1859. He reported to "Tennessee" that grazing in Carson Valley surpassed that in the Golden State.

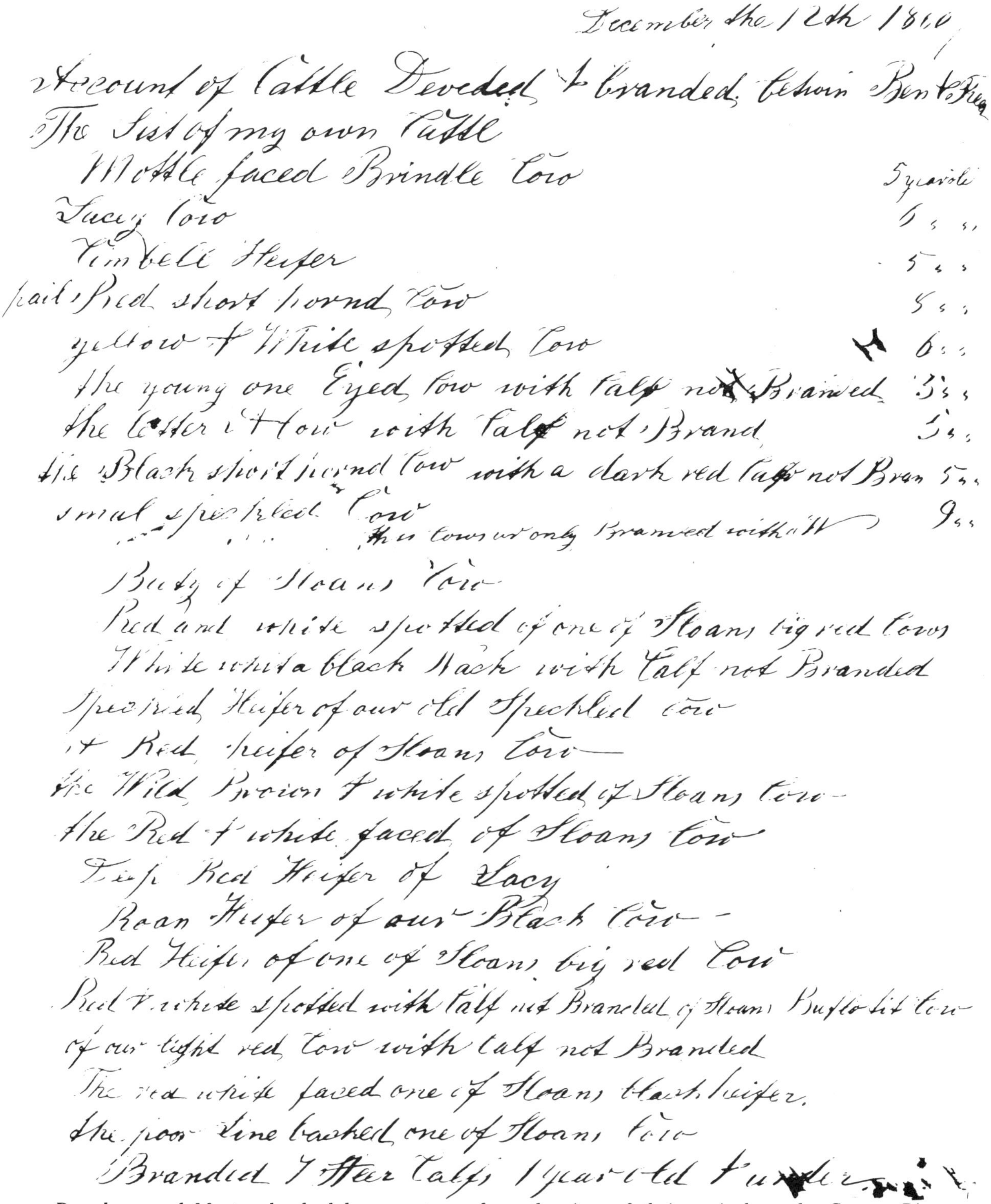

December the 12th 1860

Account of Cattle Deveded & branded betwin Ben & Fred

The List of my own Cattle

Mottle faced Brindle Cow   5 year old

Lacy Cow   6 " "

Timbell Heifer   5 " "

paile Red short horn'd Cow   8 " "

yellow & White spotted Cow   6 " "

the young one Eyed Cow with Calf not Braned   3 " "

the letter it Cow with Calf not Brand   5 " "

the Black short horn'd Cow with a dark red Calf not Bran 5 " "

smal speckled Cow   9 " "

these cows ur only Branned with a H

Butz of Sloans Cow

Red and white spotted of one of Sloans big red Cows

White with a black Nack with Calf not Branded

Speckled Heifer of our old Speckled Cow

it Red heifer of Sloans Cow —

the Wild Brown & white spotted of Sloans Cow —

the Red & white faced of Sloans Cow

the Red Heifer of Lacy

Roan Heifer of our Black Cow —

Red Heifer of one of Sloans big red Cow

Red & white spotted with Calf not Branded of Sloans Buflo tit Cow

of our light red Cow with Calf not Branded

The red white faced one of Sloans black heifer

the poor Line backed one of Sloans Cow

Branded 7 Steer Calfs 1 year old & under

Dangberg and Mast, who had been partners from the time of their arrival on the Carson River, dissolved this association when Mast decided to move to California. H. F. Dangberg's Account Book tells how they divided the cattle. A few descriptions of the cattle divided are transcribed:

December 12th 1860

Account of Cattle Devided & branded betwin Ben & Fred

The List of my own Cattle

Mottle faced Brindle Cow	5 year old
paile red short horned Cow	8 year old
the Black short horned Cow with a dark red calf not bran(ded)	5 year old

Butz (bull) of Sloans Cow
Speckled Heifer of our old Speckled Cow
the Wild Brown & white spotted of Sloans Cow
Red & white spotted with Calf not Branded of Sloans Buflo tit Cow
Branded 7 Steer Calfs 1 year old & under

Account of Cattle Devided by Ben & Fred
List of Bens Cattle
Cheery Cow
Dark Brindle Cow
the Red Cow with a white Flank
the Brown Cow
Red Stub horned Cow
Brindle Stub horned Cow
Red Cow with Twins. not Branded, 2 Calvs
Red & White spotted Cow with one horn part of another Calv not Branded
old one Eye
The wild Black & White spotted Cow
The wild red ~~~~ of Sloans Cow
The whitissh Roan of Sloans heifer
the Red Line backs with S C on the hip with Calf not Branded
Spladerdit heifer of Sloans Cow
the oldest heifer with Calf not Branded
Roany of Sloans black Cow with smal Calf not Brande
Sprackled Heifer of our Red Cow ~~~~ with the wisset Flank
Red heifer of our figgur 2 & Cow
the dark Red heifer of Sloans Cow
the Brindel of our Brown Cow
the Red poor heifer of our Cow
paile red white faced heifer of our red Stubhornd Cow
high hornd red heifer of Sloans Brindle Cow.
Braded 7 Americkan Steer Calfs for Ben

Account of Cattle Devided by Ben & Fred
List of Bens Cattle
Cheery Cow
the red Cow with a white Flank
Red Cow with Twins. not Branded 2 Calvs
Roany of Sloans black Cow with smal Calf not Brand(d)
paile red white faced heifer of our red Stubhorned Cow
high horned red heifer of Sloans Brindle Cow
Braded (branded) 7 Americkan Steer Calfs for Ben

Butz (bull) of Sloans* Cow

---
*Sloan was a stockman in the Truckee Meadows. In 1857 Dangberg pastured cattle for him.

A polled or mulley Hereford sire owned by the Fred H. Dressler ranch. *(Courtesy of Anna Neddenriep Dressler)*

Whr Aaron Mixer 5th, horned Hereford bull purchased by the Dangberg Company in 1942. *(Courtesy of Juanita Schubert)*

Scene at the annual Junior Livestock Show where Carson Valley young people frequently take prizes. *(Courtesy of Anna Neddenriep Dressler)*

Dipping cattle in control of various pests such as ticks and lice. The cattle are held in a pen then forced to swim through a warm bath of disinfectants heated by boilers. The facilities for this operation were situated on the Dangberg Ranch near the V & T Railway tracks a mile north of Minden.

Branding calves on the Scossa Ranch. *(Courtesy of James A. Lawrence)*

"Tennessee"saw the paradise and so named it. In the winter of 1859-1860, he saw that elysium turned into a graveyard as hundreds, and possibly thousands, of quadrapeds starved or froze to death during the prolonged storms and freezing weather of that year (*S.F.H.*, December 21, 1859). Hiram Mott and his son Israel, among the first settlers and grazers of cattle in Carson Valley, lost 300 head. Others, among them Henry Van Sickle, drove their cattle to the desert or to the Owens Valley where many were confiscated by the Paiute Indians, claiming trespass.

The grazing of cattle in transit, as one may say, ended after 1860 with the slowing down of the great migration. There ensued a long period when the energies of the settlers in Carson Valley were directed toward the growing, harvesting and selling of hay and grain to the near-by mining towns and to making butter and raising chickens, both for home consumption and for sale. One exception to this practice was Henry Van Sickle, proprietor of the station that bore his name, who about 1880, had five or six hundred head of cattle. Others not named had 2000. Hay and grain, however, were the principal cash crops for Carson Valley farmers until about 1890 when the declining yields of the mines, the actual closing of many, and the abandonment of towns forced them to find other cash crops.

By this time a number of the pioneer ranches had fallen into the hands of German immigrants who came to this country in the 1870s. These young men saved their earnings, patched their own clothes, knitted their own socks, and lived very frugally. By these means they soon accumulated enough money to make down payments on holdings coming on the market through estate settlements or on properties that were abandoned by their owners during the long depression following the Panic of 1873. Thus, a large number of the major farms of Carson Valley came into the hands of immigrants from the neighborhood of Verden in Hanover and of others from Schleswig-Holstein. These men, for the most part, eventually turned to dairying, the promotion of creameries and, hence the mass production of butter for their cash crop.

The German immigrants from the neighborhood of the village of Halle in Westphalia, although originally they also had dairy herds, eventually turned to the breeding and feeding of cattle and sheep. A few of these men were immigrants of the 1850s and early 1860s. Among these latter immigrants was H.F. Dangberg who had 300 or 400 head of stock in 1870. In 1890, he expanded his operation by purchasing 596 head of cattle from the Boyd estate as well as rangeland in the Pinenut Hills. In 1894, he purchased

Cattle returning in the fall from alpine ranges. They are moving north along U.S. Route 395 to Carson Valley.

650 head from Elkan Cohn who at that time was operating the Klauber Ranch. In 1896, he purchased 96 head from the Brockliss estate. All of these cattle were acquired on the depressed markets of the day for less than ten dollars per head.

That his operation was prospering may be indicated by the report that in April of 1892, Dangberg shipped cattle to Chicago which were, as one local newswriter reported, "the best that had ever gone to that market."

The type of feed available in the Pinenut Hills for these herds is described by the Surveyor General of the State of Nevada in his *Report* for 1891-1892. He said of this feed, under the caption "Grazing," that the nutritious bunch grasses of the mountains afford excellent pasturage during the summer while the succulent white sage and other herbs make excellent provender for the winter.

Fortune and their own industry and good judgment favored the German immigrants in Carson Valley. In the years following the 1890s they have prospered and exerted influence, not as a single German community, but as two separate German communities — the dairymen largely from Hanover and Schleswig-Holstein devoting their public life to the building up of the Lutheran Church — the range livestock operators largely from Westphalia going into poli-

tics. Both groups have devoted themselves to the improving of their breeding stock, led, in the case of the range live-stock operators, by the Dangberg and Dressler interests.

Prior to the end of World War I, in 1918, replacement breeding stock for triple-purpose cattle of Carson Valley — that is, beef, work oxen, and milch cows — were the Durham short-horns; these could be secured in Lake Valley where they were brought from the valleys of California for work oxen in the lumber industry and for milch cows.

In 1918, on a visit to her family in Missouri, Mrs. J.B. Dangberg saw the W.N. Collier herd of registered Herefords in Fulton. She brought home with her pictures of the cattle. In the following January the H.F. Dangberg Land and Live Stock Company sent their cattle foreman, Fritz C. Neddenriep, to Missouri to see the cattle. The result was the purchase of the foundation herd of the company's Hereford breeding stock. On this trip, Mr. Neddenriep had an order from William F. Dressler to purchase a foundation herd for him also; this he did. From these two herds there began the improvement in beef cattle of Carson Valley and the conversion of all the herds of beef and range cattle to the Hereford breed. In 1921, W.F. Dressler purchased a herd of registered polled Herefords. Since then the Dressler interests have confined their breed-

Feed wagons lined up for delivering hungry beef steers their morning ration. The Dangberg Ranches before 1950.

Cows and calves of the Dangberg Company leaving on the three-day drive to summer ranges in Alpine County, California. This photograph was chosen by the Photographic Society of America (Philadelphia) for its one hundred best print of the year schedule for 1944. *(Courtesy of Juanita Schubert)*

The first Dressler (originally spelled Droessler) home. Mr. August F. Dressler and Mrs. Dressler on the porch. *(Courtesy of Anna Neddenriep Dressler)*

Separating cows and two month old calves prior to marking and branding on the Dressler Ranch. *(Courtesy of Anna Neddenriep Dressler)*

Hereford cows on the Rocky Creek Ranch. *(Courtesy of James A. Lawrence)*

ing to perfecting this strain of Herefords. In this undertaking, Fred H. Dressler, eldest son of W.F. Dressler, has taken the lead. His devotion to improvement of Herefords, his flair for colorful expression of his conservative views on the economy have, in the last twenty years, brought him to national prominence in the cattle industry.

Taking H.F. Dangberg's place on the State Board of Stock Commissioners in 1946, Fred Dressler has continued to serve on that board. In 1944, he and F.C. Neddenriep became charter members of the Nevada Hereford Association. Dressler served as president of this association from May 1948 to June 1954. From 1949 to 1951 he was president of the Nevada State Cattle Association; from 1957 to 1962, a director of the American Hereford Association, and, from 1958 to 1959 he was a vice-president of the American Cattlemen's Association, becoming its president from 1960 to 1961. On the occasion of his retirement as president, Fred Dressler put into words his own beliefs, well-known in Carson Valley and acceptable to the national association where they contribute to the matrix of that organization's stand for constitutional government, states' rights, and private enterprise. The opening paragraph of

his farewell address is a succinct summary of these views. He said, "First, we have responsibilities as citizens, the pride, the dignity and self-respect of standing on our own two feet and not leaning on other folks for our existence. Then we have duties as cattlemen, as custodians of the lands and animals only loaned to us by a Divine Providence and the conscious or unconscious continuance of this privilege by our fellow men under the laws and government of a yet free people."

When Carson Valley ranchers elected to go into the range livestock business, they began systematic use of the public lands, accessible from their base ranches, for spring and summer grazing of livestock. This was putting the public land to productive use, involving a system of operation called technically "trans-humance." The users of public lands for the production of meat have been, since the establishment of the Forest Service in 1908 and the Grazing Service twenty-two years later in 1934, under constant pressure to curtail their use of them. The federal agencies set up to regulate its use, originally for multi-purpose activities, are presently giving priority to the preservation of fish and game. The appearance in the west in 1934 of the vanguard

126

of youthful bureaucrats sent out to implement the whims of policy dreamed up in Washington has inspired someone with amused contempt to write the following ditty:

"Here's to the gallant *Grazier*
He's been out of college a year
He knows mathematics, French and dramatics
But *what* in the h_ _ _ is a *steer*?"

With reference to the dilemma in which the range livestock industry of Carson Valley now finds itself with recreation taking precedence of all else, Fred Dressler appropriately said in his farewell address to the National Cattlemen's Association: "Recreation should never take precedence over basic necessities. Recreation can best be appreciated and most beneficial on a full stomach!"

Sheep

ON JULY 22, 1887, the *Territorial Enterprise*, calling them a "nuisance," reported the high valleys of the Sierra Nevada full of "bleating, stinking, all-devouring sheep," and rejoiced that the bears were killing them! On August 9, of the next year the same paper called the innocent-appearing sheep the "pest" of the Sierra and claimed their fires, presumably the fires of the herders, were burning the forests. Some of these objectionable quadrapeds no doubt wintered in Carson Valley where the assessor discovered at least 4500 of them in 1887 and 2000 in 1888. This unfavorable view of sheep has persisted through the years despite the fact that their early appearance in Carson Valley was under escort of none other than the admired Kit Carson. In 1853, Carson, assisted by a crew of Mexican sheepherders, drove 5000 head, brought from New Mexico, through Carson Valley and up the Carson (Woodford's) Canyon on their way to the hungry miners of California. Millwright Thomas Knott reports that William B. Thorington permitted the sheep to pass free over his toll bridge in the canyon!

In answer to the scurrilous attacks on sheep by the *Territorial Enterprise*, Robert L. Fulton, land agent of the Central Pacific Railway and also an articulate observer of nature and other phenomena, in 1890, took up the defense of these maligned animals, pointing out what owners already knew — that eight or ten sheep will thrive where one cow will live, that a sheep will produce two crops a year—wool and meat—that, in contrast to cattle, a sheep will provide these two crops in one third of the time that it takes to put meat on a beef animal that can go to market, and, finally, that the time taken to replace lost, dead, or sold sheep is one third of that required for cattle. Looking a little farther to the effect of the sheep industry on the community, Mr. Fulton sagely observed that to operate an outfit owning 5000 sheep requires the boss, two herders and a packer, all four of whom, in contrast to the one man required to utilize the same area with 500 cattle, were free spenders in the community. And last but by no means least, the railroad could look forward to shipping out both

meat and wool, and shipping in all the supplies to dip, mark and doctor them. He concluded the commercial activity associated with the running of sheep is impressive in comparison to that associated with the running of cattle. Needless to say many men in the 1890s agreed with him.

This attitude is reflected in Carson Valley where the assessor has found sheep every year from 1868 to the present. It is also reported that wool was shipped out of the valley every year from 1873 to the present. The *Carson Valley News* reported in its issue of October 30, 1885, that H.F. Dangberg had bought 5000 sheep and in its issue of February 25, 1887 that he had sold eight carloads of sheep and on the third of June of the same year, that he had sold 20,000 pounds of wool.

The assessor reported 13,000 head in Carson Valley in 1898; in 1925 he reported 25,000 head. This number wintered on Carson Valley ranches and ranged in summer on the Alpine meadows of the Sierra Nevada on both private land and on government land under permits, after its establishment, from the United States Forest Service. In spring and autumn the 25,000 to 30,000 sheep ranged on the deserts to the east of the valley. The annual clip of wool was about a quarter of a million pounds. This industry came under pressure from the United States Forest Service in the early 1930s when significant shifts in policy were instituted in Washington in the name of conservation. The pressure, amounting to confiscation in many cases, has continued until the present when but 5000 head are wintered in Carson Valley and grazed on the dependent ranges.

A lack of skilled labor has always been a problem for the sheep industry. The popular opinion, matching the contempt in which the sheep were held by the reporters on the *Territorial Enterprise*, has been that any idiot could herd sheep to which J.B. Dangberg always countered with the devastating understatement that a herder had to know more than a sheep.

In the 1890s when the industry began to expand, the records of the H.F. Dangberg Land & Live Stock Company show that H.F. Dangberg first solved the labor problem by going into partnership, in 1890, with Louis (Ludwig) Ruhenstroth — Dangberg supplying the capital and Ruhenstroth the labor. Dangberg's early entry into the sheep business may rest on his familiarity with the industry which has flourished in his native Westphalia for centuries. In 1895 Henry Luhrs, a Hanoverian, herded sheep for Dangberg. In 1896, the name of Pete Louze, a Basque from the Pyrenees, appears on the payroll, and in 1897, that of Florentine Faure. From this time onward the Basque sheepherders, coming from the Pyrenees in Spain and France, where conditions are similar to those in the western United States, became an integral part of the industry, herding for others. Some at length acquired their own bands of sheep, or retired as innkeepers.

Praise for the skill of these herders, coming from the Pyrenees, cannot be sung more effectively than by telling the story of one of them, the well-known Joe Micheo of Gardnerville who was proprietor of the popular Pyrenees Hotel until his death in 1968.

Joe was an eighteen-year-old boy when he set foot on our shores, in 1908, and took to the desert a band of 1500

Carson Valley sheep grazing in Alpine County, California. *(Courtesy of James A. Lawrence)*

head of ewes. This was in the fall when water was scarce and there was danger of early storms and even blizzards. This tall, slender lad proceeded out into the lonely desert where the only human being he could hope to see for the next three months was a camptender who came once a week with supplies and directions as to where feed for the sheep could be found. Joe had with him a donkey bearing his tent, his week's supply of food, matches, utensils and clothing, and a gun to kill marauding wild cats or coyotes. Also with him were his two dogs, well-trained Australian Shepherds or their mongrelized descendants. Into the vast silence of the desert Joe walked. The dogs barked occasionally; the bells on the fifteen sheep, which served as markers, tinkled. At the end of day as night descended, Joe cooked and ate his supper to the accompaniment of faint desert noises which enhanced the loneliness; then he knelt in prayer, and often, God forgive him, he cried himself to sleep.

Sheep grazing on pasture land in Carson Valley. *(Courtesy of James A. Lawrence)*

Sheep grazing on the desert east of the Dangberg Company's Buckeye Ranch. *(Courtesy of Juanita Schubert)*

130

This went on day after day. Fortunately no storms came; the days were crisp and clear. The 1500 sheep, according to the mathematical computations based on the fifteen belled sheep and a prescribed number of blacks, were bedded down each night. There was satisfaction in knowing that none had been lost. Pride overcame, to a certain extent, the loneliness. Joe had made several connections at the appointed weekly rendezvous with the packer.

Then came the supreme test of his skill and of the man this boy was becoming.

He arrived at the rendezvous — no packer was there and, of course, no supplies. Food was low, so were matches. There was no one to point out the land to be grazed; the way home was uncertain. Where could it be found without endangering the sheep on ranges where poison weeds might grow, or where there was no known water for either man or beast? Joe debated these hazards in agony for two days, then decided to proceed out of the desert hills by following draws leading westward. This he accomplished and when he reached the flat country he drove the sheep toward a light that he could see at night, miles to the west. After five days of walking behind the sheep, hungry and exhausted, Joe arrived at a tiny settlement with 1500 sheep, his donkey and his two dogs. Here, despite language difficulties, Joe learned that his boss had died suddenly, the packer had quit and the family had been unable to devise any means of rescue.

After a good meal and bedding down the sheep, Joe knew that he was now a man; he had proven himself and justified the faith of his employer in the ability and the integrity of his people, the Basques of Spain's and of Southern France's Pyrenees.

The problem of securing skilled labor in the west and in Carson Valley for the sheep industry was very adversely affected by the Immigration Law of 1924, setting up the quota system. This has been overcome to some extent, since 1942, when the Nevada Range Sheep Owners Association, founded by D.W. Park and J.B. Dangberg, pioneered a program for importing herders from Spain. This program has since been taken over by the Western Range Association of Fresno and now of Los Angeles.

Power

MECHANIZING THE ranches and farms of Carson Valley has been going on since, as one pioneer told it, a thrashing machine put in operation in 1857 or 1858, on the ranch of Hiram Mott, "busted" and killed his son and namesake. Another son, Israel, died, in 1863, of injuries suffered from falling in a hay press. While these ventures and disasters were being endured by a forward-looking pioneer family, hand scythes, wooden rakes and cradles were being used on other ranches and farms.

In these early years a mechanical monster, the Petaluma press, came into operation to hasten the baling of hay for hauling to the mining camps. H.F. Dangberg purchased one on April 14, 1864. On one press, an oxen team, Dick and Star, were the motor power. Hay that they had lifted in the summer by derrick to build a stack was, in autumn, winter and spring, hand-pitched down into the maw of the press, tramped down by a man as it fell, then another man closed the side gates and the gate plunger head on top. He also pulled down the top gate which compressed the hay. Baling rope, bought on spools and unwound on reels, not wire, was used to tie the bales. It was slipped through slots and tied by hand using a bowline knot. Baling started at 4:30 a.m. and continued until dark when some 15 tons of hay had been compressed into 150 bales for loading on wagons bound for the feed yards in Carson City and Virginia City, in Bodie or elsewhere.

Several self-binders for harvesting barley and oats were purchased about 1883. These were not satisfactory.

Although there was a forward-looking disposition in Carson Valley in the early days when oxen or horse power was used to supplement manpower in many farm operations, it was well into the twentieth century before steam or gasoline-powered engines were used to lighten and hasten ranch work. The Dangberg Company purchased a Best steam engine in 1905 which powered a thrashing machine. In 1915 the Dressler ranch purchased a Holt 45, a gas tractor, and from then on the larger ranchers bought Yubas, Holts and Caterpillars, all gas-powered, to use for road building, ditch digging and heavy hauling.

This spurt into the era of mechanization slowed somewhat after the end of World War I only to be resumed during World War II when man-power shortages and wartime markets provided the incentive. There was resistance to all-out mechanization by a number of ranch operators who believed the claims made for mechanization were exaggerated. The heat and the extravagance of the arguments advanced and resisted are reflected in these lines penned by an observer of the phenomenon of change:

We'll sell the cows and mechanize
   By Christopher, we'll show these guys
That a herd of bulls and Bangs reactors
   Will buy fleets of trucks and flocks of tractors;
That horses sold on program bold
   And wagons too (so we've been told)
Will bring the funds for revolution,
   In haying methods, and the solution
Of all the ills of farming life:
   Labor, buck rakes, forks, and strife.

No more will frost and drought assail us
   And prices fall and markets fail us.
With little to sell and less to trade
   We'll garner profits in the shade,
And make the laws of economics
   Look like Sunday paper comics.

With shovels and clams and angle dozers
   We'll toss up the earth and tear up the clovers,
And make a roaring, rousing din;
   Now, just you wait, 'till we begin
And the cows go out and the "cats" come in.

Gasoline engine powered thrashing machine about 1940. *(Courtesy of James A. Lawrence)*

Man power: A ranch haying crew about 1898. The "boss" John B. Dangberg, flanked by two workmen, stands above the crew.

Cutting and thrashing grain in the field with a combined harvester powered with a Best steam engine. About 1915.

The hurry-up wagon hauling meat and other supplies to the various ranches and camps on the Dangberg properties about 1915.

Plowing on the Henningsen ranch near Waterloo before 1920. *(Courtesy of Henry and Edna Frevert)*

Loading hay with a loader invented in Carson Valley about 1915.

Horse-drawn scrapers excavating the Allerman Ditch about 1905.

Oxen-powered Petaluma Hay Press about 1890. The oxen were named Tom and Jerry. *(Courtesy of Archie Millar)*

Steam engine powered thrashing machine and crew of 16 men, about 1910. *(Courtesy of Anna Neddenriep Dressler)*

Grinding barley on F.W. Stodieck Ranch in 1896. The horse operated equipment is a power sweep. From left to right: Louis Stodieck, F.W. Stodieck, William Hussman and Fritz Bohlman. *(Courtesy of Elvin and William Stodieck)*

Horse-drawn self-binders cutting grain on a 100-acre field.

She turned expectantly to the children to see how this outstanding example of manly strength and beauty would impress them. Freddie's perceptive comment was, "Where's his pants?"

Dresslerville

THE INDIAN colony at Dresslerville came into existence, after 1917, when the late W. F. Dressler, state senator from Douglas County (1919-1945), donated a forty-acre tract of bench land west of the East Fork of the Carson River to the Washoe tribe to be used by them as a settlement. Mr. Dressler acted on the request of Washoe Indians, Benny James and Captain Pete Mayo. Benny James was born in Genoa and later became a well-known guide and packer at Lake Tahoe. Rumor has it that he was often asked to be a headman of the Washoe tribe but consistently declined the honor. Slowly some of the kinship groups, living on the valley ranches where they had done seasonal work for the owners since the days of the pioneers, began to move to this land. By 1923 there were sufficient families with children present to justify the opening of a school.

One of the early teachers of these forty Washoe children of all ages and grades tells several unusual stories concerning her endeavor to make these lovable and, for the most part, eager children acquainted with the kind of education offered the young in the public school system.

Among the students was one very fat boy about fourteen years of age named Freddie who was a gentleman, a guard and a guide to his admired teacher. Freddie also took pride in seeing that no frauds were perpetrated on his smaller, less knowledgeable tribesmen.

History was, of course, one of the subjects taught — world history and United States history. Teacher took her flock in great leaps from the Stone Age through Egypt, Greece, the Roman Empire, the British Empire, the French Revolution and right down to the current administration in Washington, D.C. As a final bit of innocent indoctrination in the love of country, she told how, when a student at a school in Washington, D.C., she had the great honor of attending a reception where she shook the hand of — of all people — the President of the United States!

Teacher looked around expecting to hear "Oh's" and "Ah's." She was met with stony silence. As was her custom in situations of unexpected reaction, she turned to Freddie for an explanation. She got it! Freddie said, "I don't believe it!"

Art was another subject which seemed worthy of special emphasis and effort for these deprived children. Teacher thought long and hard of ways and means to bring the glories of Greek and European art to their attention. Surely, she thought, children with such skill in drawing, in design and such native appreciation of beauty would enjoy some of the great masterpieces of the western world. She collected cutouts of friezes from the Parthenon, of the Laocoön, and of many other masterpieces. At length came the day for exposing the children to her collection — all seemed to be going well until she came to the Apollo Belvedere.

Captain Pete Mayo of the Washoe Indians and Governor Emmett D. Boyle of Nevada. *(Courtesy of Hank Pete and George Hussman)*

Tragedy

THE WASHOE Indian Village of Dresslerville came to wide notice in the western press when, on Christmas Eve of 1947, a cabin in which a group of women, children and old men were enjoying a friendly gambling game, was burned to the ground, destroying the inmates. It was a tragedy of unbelievable horror. How it came about has never been explained to the satisfaction of relatives of the victims.

Dresslerville. *(From a water color by James A. Lawrence)*

The story begins with the fact that for many years after the Washoe Indians moved to their forty-acre preserve, in the middle 1920s, Clara Frank (or Holbrook as she was sometimes called) who was a canny business woman and one acquainted also with the gentle art of blackmail, operated a gambling house for profit. She thus capitalized on the well-known love of her people for games of chance. The cabin in which the holocaust of Christmas Eve 1947 occurred was hers.

Standing outside it on that fateful night were several young men, just out of the Army. Their separation pay had made gambling more than usually profitable to the winners for the past several days as well as to the operators of the gambling house. It is known that at this time there was a quarrel going on among the members of Clara's family over the profits of the enterprise. In the course of the quarrel, one of the young men, crazed with anger and drink, dashed into the cabin, tipped over the stove, and flung a jug of kerosene on it. An explosion followed. The fury of the flames engulfed all those present — old men, women, children. One of the old men escaped to find his way to the doctor's office in Gardnerville. He died later of his burns.

The monument on page 138 was erected by a lone woman, Mabel Washoe Filmore, who had several relatives among the victims. She has raised this monument to the memory of the thirteen who perished so needlessly on that fearful night, a reminder that heedless anger can bring great suffering and sorrow to the innocent.

137

The monument. There are three corrections to be made in the legend: The date of the fire was 1947 (not 1948); the name of the last victim does not belong here; the date of the dedication was, owing to feuding in the tribal council, delayed until July 7, 1970, when, under the sponsorship of the Carson Valley Historical Society and the Carson Valley Chamber of Commerce, an appropriate ceremony was held. *(Courtesy of Frank L. Griffin, Jr.)*

Susie

S HE LOVED children and dogs, and men loved her. She said, "Me good pfor him, me good workin'." She was just one generation removed from the time when her people had seen the first white man with his horses, his cattle and his sheep, his guns and his white bread — that bread that smelled so evilly itself and made the white man smell so vilely. However, like limburger, the taste was good. Before long it was more pleasant to do a task for the white man and eat his bread than it was to spend hours grinding and winnowing pine nuts to make the delicious native pine nut soup or pounding away in a mortar the bitter-sour acorns to make flour for biscuits. And thus a culture was replaced!

Hours spent at the wash tub, at the ironing board or scrubbing kitchen floors and washing windows provided the instruments of change; the reward received provided the dynamics. The white man's food was the love potion that drew the men. Yes, Susie knew why she was loved — it seemed perfectly natural that a man's love should be bought. There was no bitterness, no cynicism in her view but a great deal of pride. Pride resided in the fact, not that she had been desired by many, but that she was "good workin'." There was moral satisfaction that she had lovers serriatim and not, as some shameful women had, several — even four — at *one time*! This was disgusting, immoral and to be frowned upon and gossiped about.

Susie was standing at the ironing board; we had been gossiping. I asked, "Susie, how many men you got altogether?" She paused, set the iron on end and began counting on her fingers, "Pfirst me gottum Sammy's Pfadder;" the index finger went down. "Nen me gottum Johnny;" the middle finger went down. She paused for several minutes. "Nen me gottum one me pforgettum dat name!" The ring finger went down. "Nen me gottum Johnson." She doubled down the little finger. "Next time me gottum Martin, nen me gottum Johnny Christensen, nen Bill and now me gottum Aa-lbert," she said with delicious pride, as she tolled off the last name on the little finger of her left hand. "Eight!" she said, triumphantly.

Susie. (© *James A. Lawrence*)

139

Appendix

Sam Brown

THE SHOOTING of bad man Sam Brown on the evening of July 6, 1861, by Henry Van Sickle, whose life he had threatened earlier on that day, has drawn the attention of writers out of all proportion to the importance of the event in the annals of Carson Valley. Brown was on his way from Carson City to Aurora when he stopped at the Van Sickle Station near the foot of Kingsbury Grade to make his attempt on the life of the proprietor. The attempt failed and Brown proceeded on his way. Van Sickle pursued him, passed him when he stopped at a ranch, and was standing in the door of the Lute Olds barn when Brown rode up to stop for the night. Van Sickle shot him.

These facts are recorded by Angel (1881), by Van Sickle himself in 1884 and by a reporter to the *Sacramento Daily Union,* July 8, 1861.

Much has been made of the incident since Sam P. Davis published his story (*History,* 1913). Following the account of William M. Stewart (*Reminiscences,* 1908) and relating it to the Senator's account of an encounter with Brown in a court action at Devil's Gate Toll House in the vicinity of Virginia City, Davis, with true dramatic instinct, compresses the two in time and space. He transfers the court scene to Genoa and has it occur on the same day as the attempt to shoot Van Sickle and the shooting of Brown. He makes Van Sickle, a native of New Jersey of Dutch descent, a "German" rancher, the well-known Van Sickle Station becomes "a sort of wayside inn" and the Lute Olds barn "a spot" where Brown would have to pass. It makes interesting reading.

George D. Lyman (*Saga of the Comstock Lode,* 1934) comes along and does some more dramatizing. Following Stewart and Davis and even citing Angel in his notes, a procedure which leads the casual reader to suppose that his is an historical account, he spins a yarn that makes Senator Stewart and bad man Brown rivals for the title of "chief" or "king" of the Comstock. In the course of his story he has Stewart confront Brown at the Devil's Gate Toll House and again at Genoa. After being worsted in Genoa, Lyman has Brown flee to his familiar stamping ground on the Comstock only to be shot along the road by Van Sickle.

These dramatized tales have come full cycle in the account of Robert Laxalt (*Nevada,* in States of the Nation Series, 1970, shelved in libraries for use by children) who follows Davis and Lyman, adding to their accounts the statement that Van Sickle shot Brown outside a cabin near Carson City which is twenty miles north of the actual place of the shooting.

In order that the accounts of Angel, Van Sickle and the reporter, in 1861, may be verified by another contemporary we reprint here the following signed by someone using the name "Pony" who, we suggest, may have been the Captain R.D. or Richard Watkins, whose account of the Paiute War of 1860 Angel used (p. 153, note); Watkins settled in Mono County in late 1861 where he was reported to have been a Pony Express rider.

"Now that the press of Western Nevada is busy in accounting for the mysterious disappearance of Henry Vansickle,* it will not, I think, be out of place to say something of the noted desperado Sam Brown, whose name is so often connected with that of Vansickle from the fact that it was the latter who rid the world, and especially Nevada, of Sam's generally unwelcome presence. My business in the mountains in 1860-61 made me acquainted with nearly all who were on the road between Virginia City and Placerville at that time, so of course I knew Sam Brown. In fact he once did me a great favor — a favor which many a better man would not have done. I had ridden from 'Yank's' through very deep snow, and on reaching 'Friday's' Station found that my horse was entirely given out while I had yet to cross the summit to Genoa before getting a change. 'Friday' (Burke) had neither horse nor mule at home, and I was about to take to the Norwegian skates when Sam came from the stable with his famous grey mare saying, 'Leave her at your stable in Genoa and I will get yours through tomorrow,' which he did. I tell this lest the reader may think while reading the rest of the sketch that I was rather too intimate with so notorious a man.

"I think it was on the 6th of July, '61 that Sam Brown, who had killed eleven men, and said he wanted another to make it an even dozen, himself got killed by Henry Vansickle. The writer on that morning was in front of Wells, Fargo & Co.'s office in Carson City, waiting for Sam Hamilton who was due from the East with the Pony Express. Hamilton soon hove in sight with another horseman by his side, who from his long, flowing hair I soon recognized as Sam Brown. They came thundering across the plaza neck and neck up to the express office. While Hamilton and I were changing his saddle to another horse I asked him why he came into town with such a partner. And he said that he could not help it — that Brown joined him at Empire with his horse fresh while his horse 'Spider' had run from Dayton, 'and by _ _ _ _, Pony I couldn't get away from him.' Hamilton soon sped away West on a fresh horse and Brown laughed till the tears came telling me how he had played Sam H. the pony rider. Sam stayed in Carson until three or four o'clock in the afternoon drinking and chatting with seeming friends, for none dared to seem otherwise than friendly to his face, and then said that he was going to Aurora and would go as far as Lute Olds' that night. I thought of Vansickle and tried to dissuade him, knowing that every time he was in liquor he swore to have Van's scalp. Here I will inform the reader of the trouble between Brown and Vansickle and the reason for it.

"About a year before, Brown having killed a man in Virginia, found it so hot that he concluded to take a trip to California for his health. He was closely pursued by the murdered man's friends one of whom borrowed Van's pistol from the barkeeper, George Brobecker, with which to hunt Brown. On his return a few months later Sam learned

---

*Van Sickle reappeared, see the *Genoa Weekly Courier*, June 5, 1885

this fact, and although Van disclaimed all knowledge of the loaning of the pistol, Brown when drunk would always be hunting for him and would certainly have killed him had not Van by good luck got the drop on Sam. That was why I tried to dissuade Sam from his trip to Aurora that day knowing that he had to pass Van's and would probably kill him if he saw him. It was of no use, however; he was bound to go and asked me to go with him to Tim Smith's stable after his mare, and I did so. Why did I go? does the reader ask. Well, you see, I knew Sam Brown and it is very evident that the reader who would question me thus was not intimately acquainted with the gentleman. He had done me the greatest favor he would — loaned me the only thing he ever loved, his grey mare; and if I had ever seemed to shun his society my life would not have been worth a counterfeit 80-cent dollar even though it had been insured for $10,000 in gold coin in every office on the coast. So I went to the stable and saw him start on his last ride, feeling that something was going to happen. And something did happen.

"What I have written, Mr. Editor, was from my own knowledge. What comes next is from disinterested third party. Wiley, the overland stage driver, came into Carson that night and said that he met Sam about half way between that place and Genoa chasing a lot of Washoe Indians. He did not seem to want to hurt them but only frighten them. He arrived at Vansickle's just before dark and rode up to the water trough at the corner of the house and not more than ten feet from the door of the barroom. Van came to the door and very politely — everybody was polite to Sam — invited him to dismount and come in. 'No,' said Sam, 'you d _ _ _ _, I have come to kill you,' and went for his pistol. Van did not stand on the order of going, but went at once for his shot gun which he always kept loaded for such an emergency. Sam followed him to the dining room door where he saw some eight or ten of Van's cowboys eating supper. Sam took in the situation at a glance and knew that it was not a good time to kill his twelfth man, and was on his mare and away like a well trained pony rider. Van was now fully awakened to the fact that something had to be done, and that it must not be put off. Gathering his cowboys and a few outside volunteers and mounting them, he started on the trail. It was now dark, and as soon as they caught a glimpse of the grey mare they opened fire but did no damage except slightly wounding the mare. Sam turned off the road and stopped at Mott's ranch, rightly thinking his pursuers would go on to Lute Olds. Mott, however, knowing his customer, refused to keep him or even open the door, and Sam was obliged to go to Olds' place and rely on his prowess and former good luck. For once luck was against him. Van's party reached Olds' Station and learning that Sam had not arrived secreted themselves advantageously and waited. They had not long to wait before the same arrived. Sam rode up very cautiously and reconnoitered the premises, when Van stepped from behind the barn door and literally filled his breast with buckshot. That was the last of one of the most noted desperados of modern times. His last words were, 'Van, you _ _ _ _, you've got me.' The next day the remains were brought to Genoa and an inquest held the result of which was that 'Sam Brown's body had been filled with lead by Henry Vansickle, and that it served him right.'

"A few words about Sam's antecedents and I am done. The next day after the killing the writer was talking with J. Neely Johnson at the Frisbie House in Carson City. Johnson knew Sam in California and knew his parents in Ohio. His father was a respectable country tavern keeper in the State of Ohio. Sam had served a term of two years and a half in San Quentin for killing his first man, and his term was out while Johnson was Governor, and he (Johnson) wrote to Sam's father to know what to do with him at the expiration of his term. The old gentleman replied that he should give him a ticket for home with money for expenses. The Governor told Sam that he was ready to do as his father requested, but Sam would have none of it. He had gone too far and liked the country too well to return to Ohio."

/signed/
"Pony"

Bibliography

In 1967, the Carson Valley Historical Society began the collection of materials on the history of Carson Valley for deposit in the Henry Van Sickle collection. The collection was founded by Jack Van Sickle and is presently shelved in the Douglas County Public Library in Minden. Various items to be found in this collection are followed by the abbreviation VSC.

The political history of Carson Valley is covered in the histories of Nevada as follows:

ANGEL, MYRON, History of Nevada. Thompson and West, Oakland, 1881. (Reproduced in facsimile, with an introduction by David F. Myrick, by Howell-North, Berkeley, 1958). The complete *Index* to this work by Helen J. Poulton was published by the University of Nevada Press, Reno, Nevada, 1966.

BANCROFT, HUBERT HOWE, The Works of Hubert Howe Bancroft, Volume XV, History of Nevada, Colorado, and Wyoming, 1840-1888. San Francisco, 1890.

SCRUGHAM, JAMES GROVES, editor, Nevada. Chicago and New York, 1935. The American Historical Society, Inc. 3 vols.

KOONTZ, JOHN, Political History of Nevada. Fifth Edition, Carson City, Nevada, 1965.

The primary source for the history of Carson Valley is the official records of Douglas County which has embraced Carson Valley since the setting up of the territorial government in 1861. Before this date and beginning in the year of first permanent settlement are the First Records of Carson Valley, Utah Ter., 1851 with entries from November 12, 1851 to March 5, 1855 (published in facsimile in *Nevada Historical Society Quarterly*, 9: 2, 3, 1966) and the so-called Kinsey's Records, copied for Douglas County from the Records of the Probate Court of Carson County, Utah Territory (Book 1, Miscellaneous, for the period October 18, 1855-July 9, 1861 and Book A, Deeds and Mortgages for the period March 3, 1856-September 15, 1861). Thus it may be seen that records for Carson Valley are continuous from 1851 to 1861 when the official records of Douglas County begin. The listing which follows of the principal records of Douglas County in the order of the first entries gives an interesting perspective on the priorities of the pioneers:

Mining Records, Book A (January 20, 1860)
Deeds, Book A (December 20, 1861)
Commissioners Minutes (December 28, 1961)
Register of Actions and Probate Court Records (December 30, 1861)
Minutes of the Probate Court (February 6, 1862)
Record of Marriages, Book A (February 11, 1862)
Court Minutes (February 17, 1862)
Miscellaneous, Book A (September 20, 1862 — December 10, 1872; Book B, 1887)
Agreements and Leases and Bills of Sale (December 19, 1862)
Mortgages, Book B (February 4, 1863)
Fictitious Persons (December 12, 1863)
Patents in Book 1 of Kinsey's Records page 355 (September 15, 1864)
Assessment Rolls (1865)
Homesteads, Book A (April 1, 1882)
Record of Deaths, Book A (May 7, 1887)
Record of Births, Book A (June 9, 1887)

Contemporary accounts including diaries, letters, and recollections of travelers over the Carson River Route and of first settlers in Carson Valley carry the record back to 1848. A few of these have been published and are listed below; others are available from the Bancroft Library (University of California, Berkeley) and from the Utah Historical Records Survey, Federal Writers Project, Salt Lake City. Both institutions have graciously accorded us copies of these when requested. There are a hundred more noted by Robert A. Armstrong in his Preliminary Union Catalog of Nevada Manuscripts (University of Nevada Library, Nevada Library Association, Reno, Nevada, 1967) for the most part deposited in libraries in California. These have not been seen. A list of those seen follows:

BEATIE, HAMPTON SIDNEY, "The First in Nevada," *Nevada State Historical Society Papers*, 1(1913-1916), pp. 168-171. VSC.

BIGLER, HENRY W., (Diary, July 22-September 28, 1848), Utah Historical Records Survey, Federal Writers Project. VSC.

BLACKBURN, ABNER, (Diary, pages 2-42-43, 2-62-64, 2-67, 2-77-78 of manuscript in Bancroft Library, copied with permission of Robert A. Allen. VSC.

BOWLES, SAMUEL, Our New West, Records of Travel between the Mississippi River and the Pacific Ocean. Hartford Publishing Co., Hartford; J.D. Dennison, New York; J.A. Stoddard, Chicago, Ill., 1870. On Carson River Route via Kingsbury Grade, pp. 308-311.

BROWN, JOHN ROSS, "A Peep at Washoe," *Nevada State Historical Society Papers*, 5(1925-1926), pp. 3-115. On Carson Valley, pp. 44-45. VSC.

CRADLEBAUGH, WILLIAM M., "Nevada Biography," The *Same*, 1(1913-1916), pp. 174-176. VSC.

DECKER, PETER, THE DIARIES OF, Overland to California in 1849 and Life in the Mines, 1850-1851. Edited by Helen S. Giffen, Georgetown, California, 1966. The Talisman Press.

DE GROOT, HENRY, Sketches of the Washoe Silver Mines, with a Description of the Soil, Climate and Mineral Resources of the Country East of the Sierra. San Francisco, 1860. At end of Kelly's First Directory of Nevada Territory. 24 pages. On Carson Valley, pp. 10-11. VSC.

HAINES, JAMES W., Life and Experiences in California and Nevada. (Excerpts copied from microfilm in Bancroft Library). VSC.

HUNTINGTON, O. B., A Trip to Carson Valley. In Eventful Narratives in the Thirteenth Book of the Faith-Promoting Series. Salt Lake City, Utah, 1887. On Carson Valley, pp. 86-87. VSC.

HUTCHINGS, JAMES MASON, Scenes of Wonder and Curiosity from Hutchings' California Magazine, 1856-1861, edited by R.R. Olmstead. Howell-North Books, Berkeley, 1962. On Carson Valley, p. 307. VSC.

JENNINGS, WM., "Carson Valley," *Nevada State Historical Society Papers*, (1913-1916), pp. 178-183.

KILGORE, WILLIAM H., The Kilgore Journal of an Overland Journey to California in the Year 1850. Edited by Joyce Rockwood Muench. Hastings House, New York, 1949. On Carson Valley, pp. 54-55. VSC.

KNOTT, THOMAS, Reminiscences. Early History of Nevada. Edited with commentary by H.H. Hamlin. The Pioneer Press of Placerville, California, 1947. On Carson Valley, passim. VSC.

LOOMIS, LEANDER V., A Journal of the Birmingham Emigrating Company, edited by Edward M. Ledyard. Salt Lake City, Utah, 1928. On Carson Valley, pp. 114-115. VSC.

McQUIG, JOHN, "The Diary of John McQuig," *Nevada Historical Society Quarterly*, 6:2 (1963), pp. 2-27. On Carson Valley, pp. 26-27. VSC.

MENEFEE, ARTHUR M., "Travels Across the Plains, 1857," The *Same*, 9:1(1966), pp. 1-28. On Carson Valley, pp. 27-28.

PLATT, P. L. & N. SLATER, Traveller's Guide across the Plains on the Overland Route to California. Reprinted from 1852 edition. Berkeley, 1963. John-Howell Books. On the Carson River Route, pp. 28-29. VSC.

REESE, JOHN, "Mormon Station," *Nevada State Historical Society Papers*, 1(1913-1916), pp. 186-190. VSC.

REMY, JULES and JULIUS F. BRENCHLEY, A Journey to Great Salt Lake City, London, 1861. 2 vols. On Carson Valley, vol. 1, pp. 32-37. VSC.

TAYLOR, BAYARD, Eldorado, being a true facsimile of the whole of the first 1850 edition . . . with biographical introduction by Richard H. Dillon. Palo Alto, 1968. Lewis Osborne. 2 vols. On Carson Valley vol. 1, p. 223; vol. 2, pp. 40-42. VSC.

VAN SICKLES (sic) HENRY, "Utah Desperadoes," *Nevada State Historical Society Papers*, 1(1913-1916), pp. 190-193. VSC.

WASSON, WARREN, "Letters of Warren Wasson, Indian Agent," Introduction by Ferol Egan, *Nevada Historical Society Quarterly*, 12:3(1969) pp. 1-26. VSC.

WOOD, JOHN, "Along the Emigrant Trail . . . diary of John Wood written in 1850," *Motor Land*, April, 1929, pp. 14-32. On Carson Valley, p. 15. VSC.

YAGER, "The Yager Journals: Diary of a Journey across the Plains (1863)," annotated by Everett W. Harris and Walt Mulcahy, Part V, *Nevada Historical Society Quarterly*, 14:1(1971), pp. 27-54. On Carson Valley, pp. 37-38. VSC.

Further accounts of the Carson River Route and Carson Valley in the 1850s are provided in records of survey parties, as follows:

DAY, SHERMAN, Report, on the immigrant wagon road explorations, September 20, 1855. Annual Report of the Surveyor General of California. Document No. 5, Senate Session of 1856, pp. 77-88. VSC.

GODDARD, GEORGE HENRY, Report of a survey of a portion of the old Carson and Johnson immigrant roads over the Sierra Nevada. The *Same*, pp. 88-186. VSC.

POWERS, O. B., Report on the Calaveras route. A trip to Carson Valley. The *Same*, pp. 187-191.

SIMPSON, JAMES H., Report of Explorations across the Great Basin of the Territory of Utah for a Direct Wagon-Route from Camp Floyd to Genoa in Carson Valley, in 1859. Washington, D.C., 1876. On Carson Valley, pp. 25-26, 91-96. VSC.

A perspective on affairs in Carson Valley in the early sixties may be gained from certain statutes: See Laws of the Territory of Nevada, First Regular Session (San Francisco, 1862) and Second Regular Session (Virginia, 1863).

Three directories of Nevada, published in the 1860s, have informative sections on Douglas County and Carson Valley:

KELLY, J. WELLS, First Directory of Nevada, San Francisco, 1862. (facsimile, The Talisman Press, Los Gatos, California, 1962), VSC.

_____, Second Directory, Virginia, 1863.

GILLIS, WILLIAM R., Nevada Directory for 1868-1869. San Francisco, 1868.

Court records furnish contemporary accounts of people and events in Carson Valley from 1851-1900. This is particularly true of the suits involving water rights on the Carson River:

CASE 520. In the District Court of the United States, Ninth District of Nevada. The Union Mill and Mining Company, Complainant vs. H.F. Dangberg, et al, Defendants. Filed September 11, 1889. (typed transcript of evidence), VSC.

CASE 12,857. In the Circuit Court of the United States, Ninth Circuit, Northern District of California John Anderson et al, Complainants, vs. Henry Bassman, et al, Respondents. Filed December, 1899. (testimony on eight microfilm reels), VSC.

Reports of the Surveyor General (1865-1900) often incorporated first hand accounts of Conditions in Douglas County, hence Carson Valley. VSC.

Reports of the State Superintendent of Public Instruction (1864) are a fruitful source of information on the schools of Douglas County, hence Carson Valley.

Census of the inhabitants of the State of Nevada, 1875. In Appendix to Journals of Senate and Assembly of the Eighth Session of the Legislature of the State of Nevada, Carson City, 1877. 2 vols. Douglas County, vol. 1, pp. 16-69. VSC.

In the 1850s newspapers in California frequently published accounts of activities on the Carson River Route and conditions and events in Carson Valley. Issues of the *San Francisco Herald,* from January 1, 1853 through October 9, 1862, have provided a number of reports. Copies of these are in the Van Sickle Collection. Other California newspapers, e.g., the *Alta California* and the *Sacramento Union,* published reports for this early period. They have, however, not been systematically examined.

Newspapers published in Nevada reported from time to time on affairs in Carson Valley. These have been consulted on specific events. They are the *Territorial Enterprise*, the first issue published in Genoa on December 18, 1858 (moving from there to Carson City in 1859 and to Virginia City in 1860), and the *Carson Daily Appeal*, first published in 1865. In 1870 this paper became the *Register*, in 1872, the *New Daily Appeal* and from 1874, the *Daily Appeal*.

Newspapers published in Carson Valley are shelved in the office of the recorder of Douglas County in issues dated as follows:

Carson Valley News, from February 20, 1875 through July 16, 1880.

Genoa Courier or *Weekly Courier*, from July 23, 1880 through May 26, 1899, when its plant was removed to Gardnerville.

Courier or *Weekly Courier*, Gardnerville, January 5, 1900 through March 4, 1904.

Record, Gardnerville, January 3, 1901-March 4, 1904.

Record Courier, Gardnerville, March 11, 1904 to date.

For further information on the newspapers of Carson Valley, see Richard E. Lingenfelter, 1858-1958, The Newspapers of Nevada, a History and Bibliography, with an Introduction by David F. Myrick. San Francisco, 1964. John-Howell Books.

Articles and books on the history of Carson Valley and the Carson Valley Route:

ASHBAUGH, DON, Nevada's Turbulent Yesterday. Westernlore Press, 1963. On Carson River Route, pp. 84-86, 88-92.

BROOKS, JUANITA, "The Mormons in Carson County, Utah Territory," *Nevada Historical Society Quarterly*, 8:1(1965) pp. 5-25.

CHALFANT, W. A., The Story of Inyo. Pinon Book Store. Bishop, California, 1933. (First copyright, 1922). On Carson Valley cattle in Inyo County, 1860, pp. 141, 148.

DANGBERG, GRACE, Washoe Tales. Occasional Paper, Nevada State Museum, Carson City, Nevada, 1968.

ELLIOT, RUSSELL R., "Nevada's First Trading Post: A Study in Historiography," *Nevada Historical Society Quarterly*, 13:4(1970) pp. 3-10.

FARQUHAR, FRANCIS P., History of the Sierra Nevada. University of California Press, Berkeley and Los Angeles in collaboration with the Sierra Club, 1965. On Carson River Route, pp. 93, 97-102.

GEORGETTA, CLEL, Golden Fleece in Nevada, Reno, 1972. Venture Publishing Company, Ltd. On Carson Valley, pp. 280, 286-293, 435-437.

GOODWIN, VICTOR O., "Development of Emigrant Routes of Northern Nevada," *Nevada Historical Society Quarterly*, 8:3-4(1965), pp. 25-41. On Carson Valley, p. 29.VSC.

GREEVER, WILLIAM S., The Bonanza West. University of Oklahoma Press, Norman, 1963. On Carson Valley and Kingsburgy Grade, pp. 145-150.

KANE, DORIS, "James Kane's Stageline," *Frontier Times*, July, 1964, pp. 6-10, 46-49. VSC.

KRICK, GROVER, "Douglas County Court House," *Nevada State Bar Journal*, 1:3(1939), pp. 227-233. VSC.

MACK, EFFIE MONA, "John A., Snowshoe Thompson, Hero of the Sierras," *Nevada Magazine*, August, 1945. Condensed with material added by Paul Knudsen and published in *Sons of Norway*, May and June, 1956.

MALLOY, WILLIAM DOYLE, Carson Valley, 1852-1860. Unpublished M.A. thesis, University of California, Berkeley, 1931. Microfilm. VSC.

MAULE, WILLIAM, A Contribution to the Geographic and Economic History of the Carson, Walker and Mono Basins in Nevada and California. California Region Forest Service. U.S. Department of Agriculture. San Francisco, California, 1938. On Carson Valley, passim. VSC.

MENZEL, FREDERICK, History of the Trinity Evangelical Lutheran Church, Gardnerville, Nevada, 1920. VSC.

MILLER, EUNICE, "The Timber Resources of Nevada," *Nevada State Historical Society Papers*, 5(1925-1926) pp. 375-457.

MITCHELL, STEWART, "Crossing the Sierra," *California Highways and Public Works*, Centennial edition, September 9, 1950, pp. 49-68. Maps. VSC.

MORGAN, DALE L., The Humboldt, Highroad of the West. New York, 1943. Farrar & Rinehart, Incorporated. On Carson River Route, pp. 198-207 and passim.

SCHAEFER, JACK, Heroes Without Glory. Boston, 1965. Houghton Mifflin Company, The Riverside Press. On John A. Thompson, pp. 55-93.

SELKIRK, BERT, Editor, Gardnerville. Published by the *Record Courier*, Gardnerville, Nevada, 1909. VSC.

STEWART, GEORGE RIPLEY, The California Trail. New York, 1962. McGraw-Hill Book Company, Inc. On the Carson River Route, pp. 197-200, 205-207, 288.

THOMAS, BENJAMIN E., "The California-Nevada Boundary," *Annals of the Association of American Geographers*. 42(March, 1952) pp. 51-68. VSC.

VANDENBURG, WILLIAM O., Placer mining in Nevada. Bulletin of Nevada State Bureau of Mines and the Mackay School of Mines (University of Nevada Bulletin XXX, May 15, 1936, on Carson Valley, pp. 68-69.

WHITE, CHARLES LEE, "Surmounting the Sierras, the Campaign for a Wagon Road," *Quarterly of the California Historical Society*, 7:1(March, 1928) pp. 3-19.

WINTHER, OSCAR OSBURN, Express and Stagecoach Days in California, Palo Alto, 1938. Stanford University Press. On Carson Valley, pp. 158-159. VSC.

WRIGHT, WILLIAM (Dan De Quille), "Snow-shoe Thompson," *The Overland Monthly*, 8(October, 1886) pp. 419-435.

Unpublished biographies and reminiscences, letters, surveys:

BROCKLISS, MARMADUKE, History and Genealogy of the Brockliss Family. Typescript dated Gardnerville, 1949. VSC.

BROWN, NORMAN D., Reminiscences, Early Days of Carson Valley. Transcribed from tape recording made in 1962. VSC.

CARSON VALLEY HISTORICAL SOCIETY, German Immigrants and Early Settlers in Carson Valley, Survey, Ms. VSC.

_____, British Immigrants and Early Settlers in Carson Valley, Survey, Ms., VSC.

DANGBERG, GRACE and BEATRICE JONES, The Motts of Mottsville. 1972. VSC.

DANGBERG, H. F., Diaries, 1863-1872; Account books, 1856-1900. Letters to and from Germany, 1856-1860. In private collection.

DES ISLES, ISAAC, Letters from Sheridan, Nevada, 1865-1866. Typescript. VSC.

FAY, ERNIE, Recollections of Carson Valley. Transcript of tape recording made in 1965. VSC.

KLAUBER, ABRAHAM, Life of Abraham Klauber in Nevada and Carson Valley, 1859-1869. Copy of pp. 17-22 of complete manuscript. VSC.

LUTHER, MARK LEE, Early Life of Ira Manley Luther. N.P., N.D., Photocopy of original. VSC.

NEBEKER, MARGARET ESTELLA EGBERT, compiler. Descendants of David Park and Ann Brooks Park. N.P., N.D. (about 1950). In private collection.

PARK, DAVID and MORTON GRAY, Reminiscences of Genoa and Carson Valley. Transcript of tape recording made in 1963. VSC.

THOMPSON, J. A. ("Snowshoe"), Copies of two letters from Washington, D.C., dated February 6, and March 7, 1872. VSC. Originals in collection of Miss Lillian Bergevin.

Index